I0432570

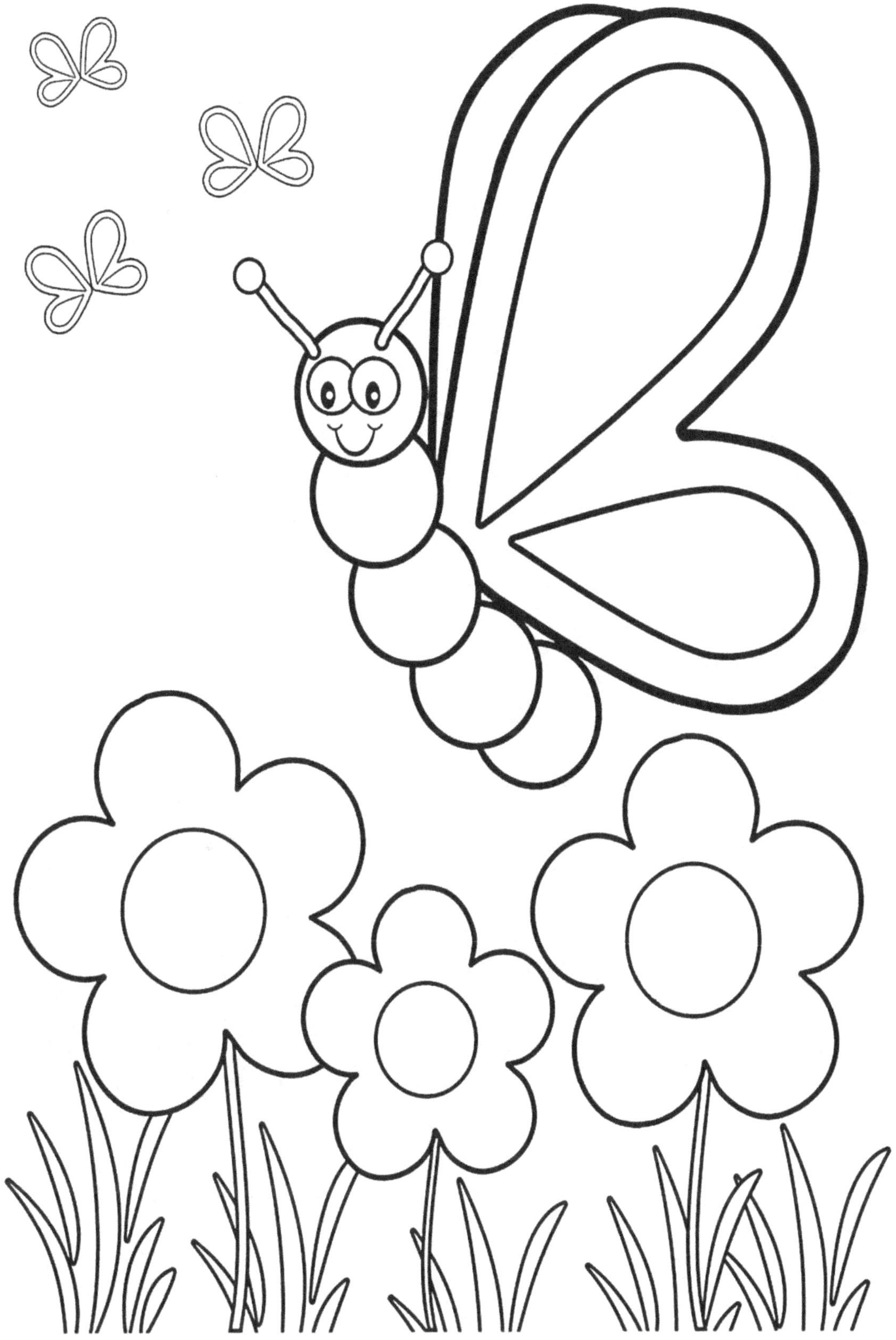

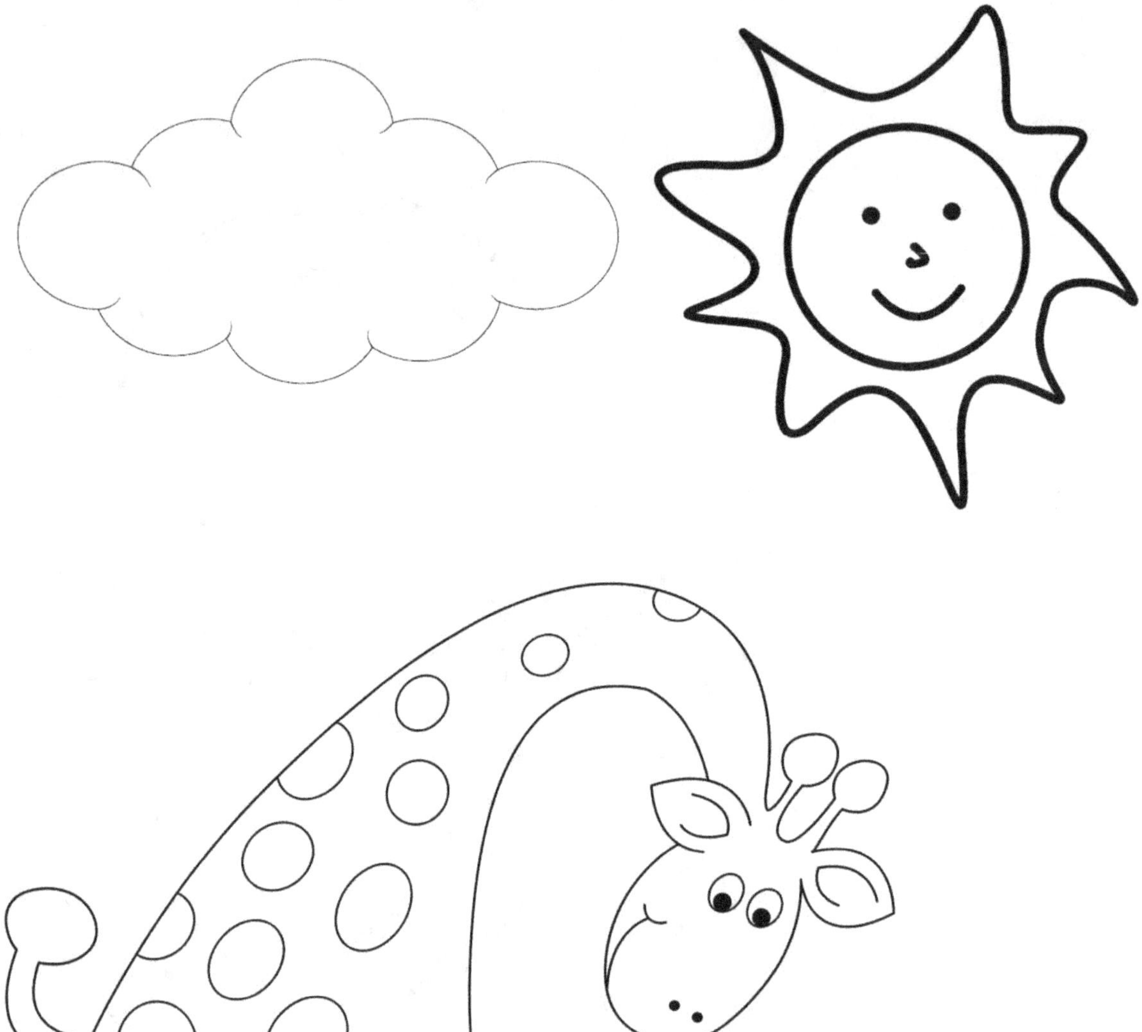

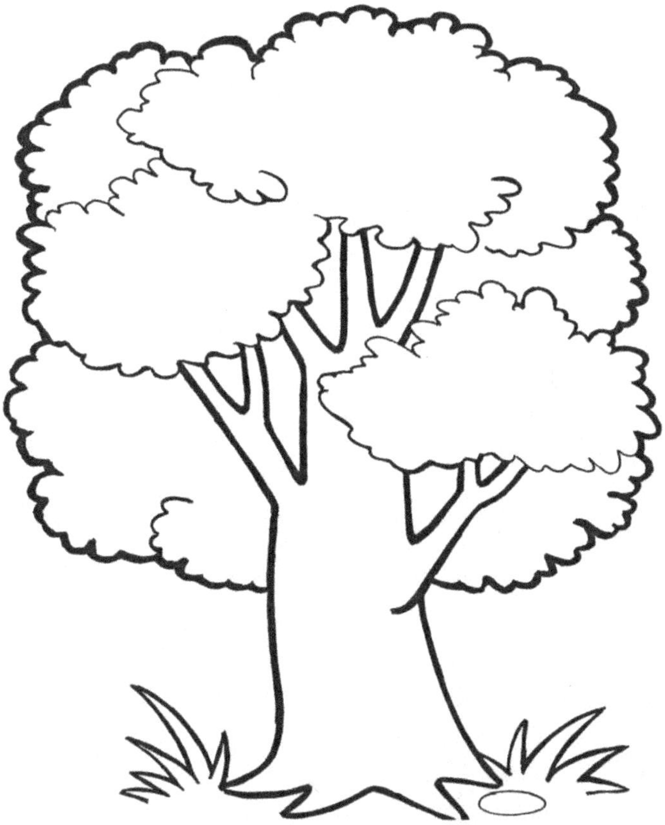

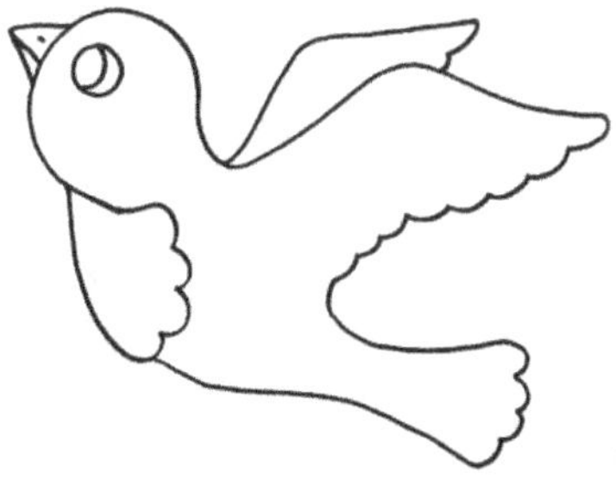

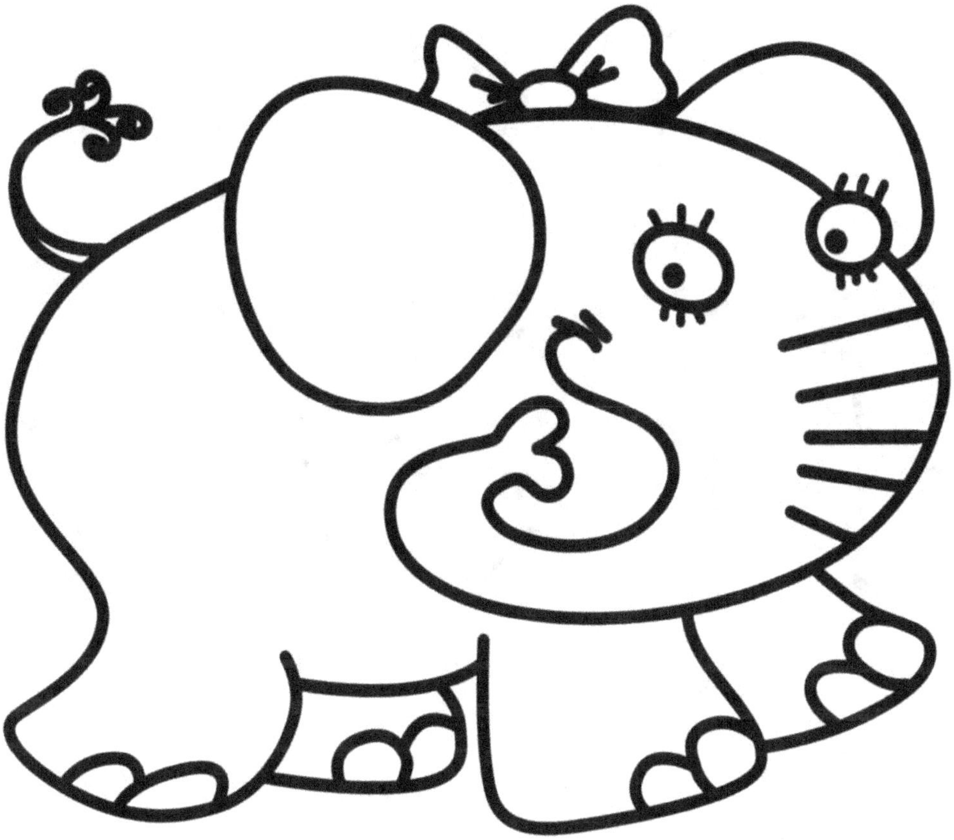

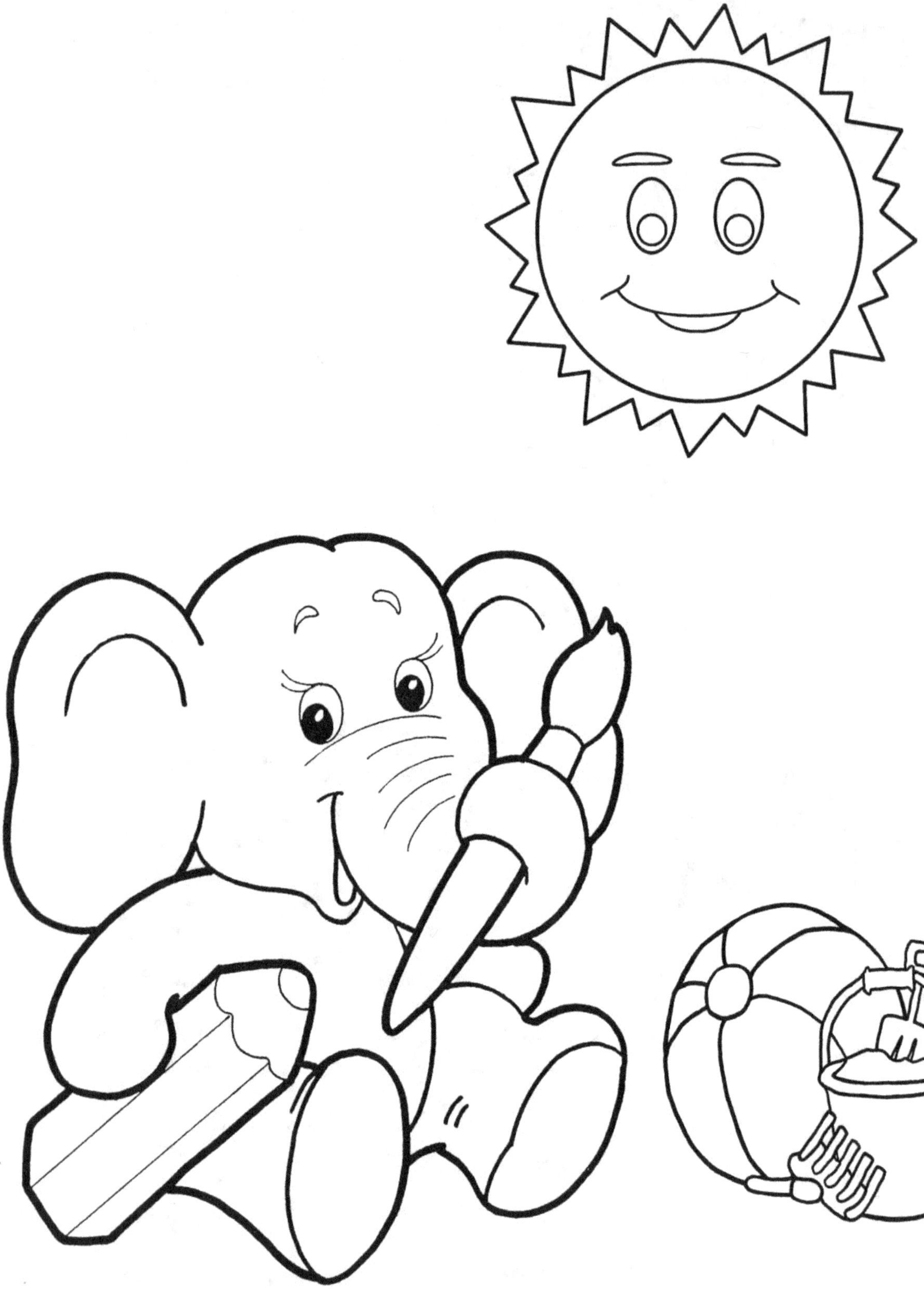

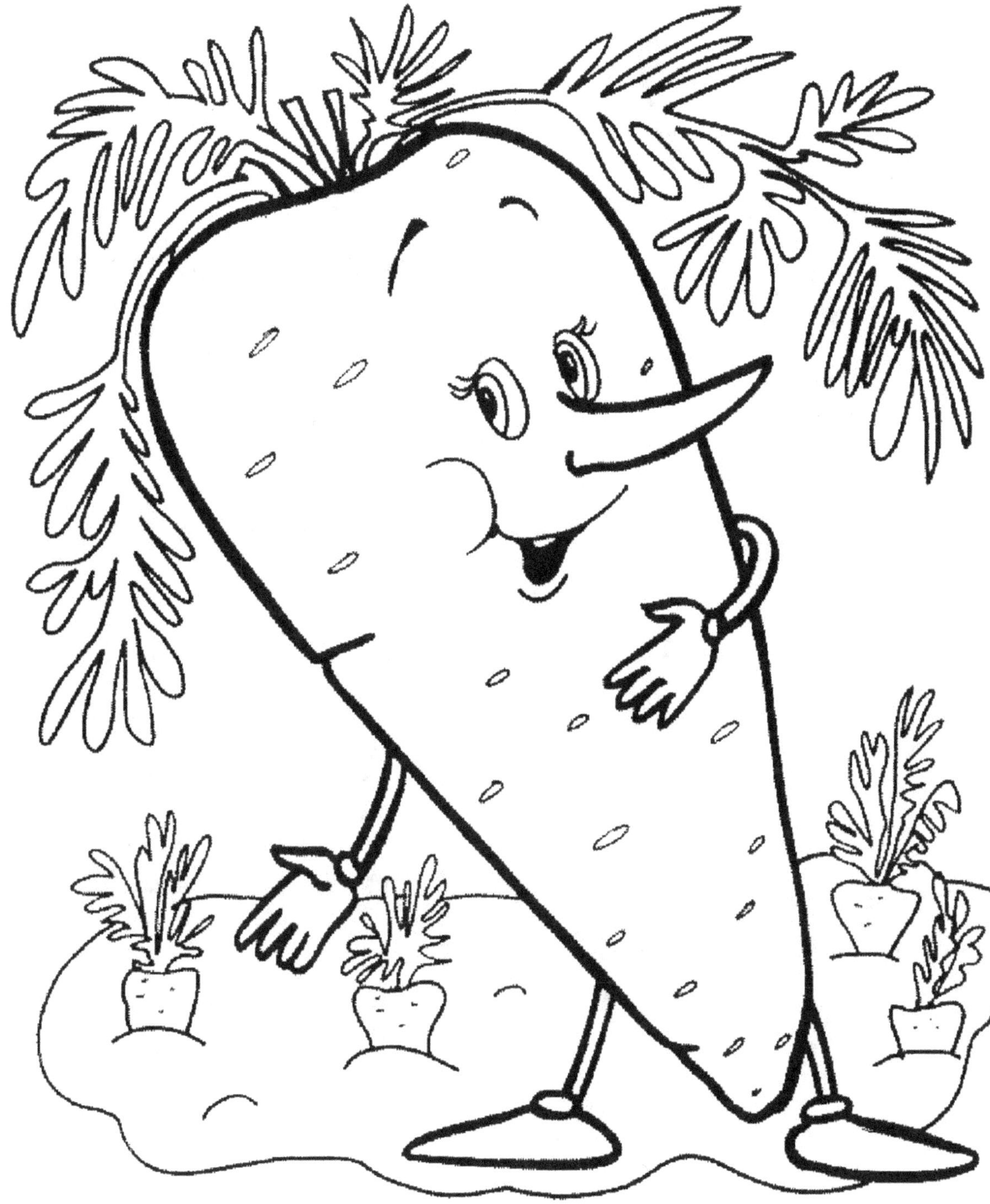

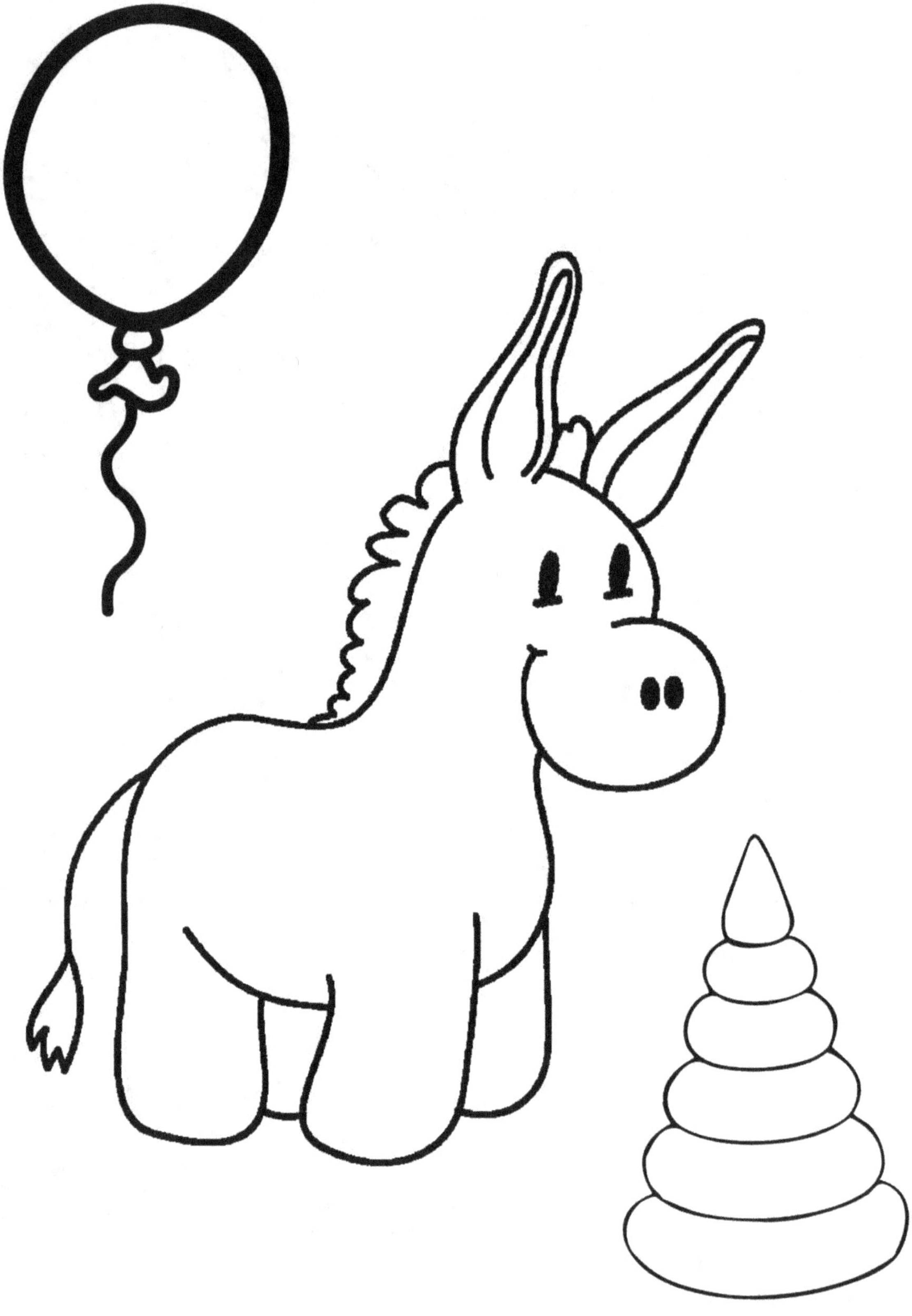

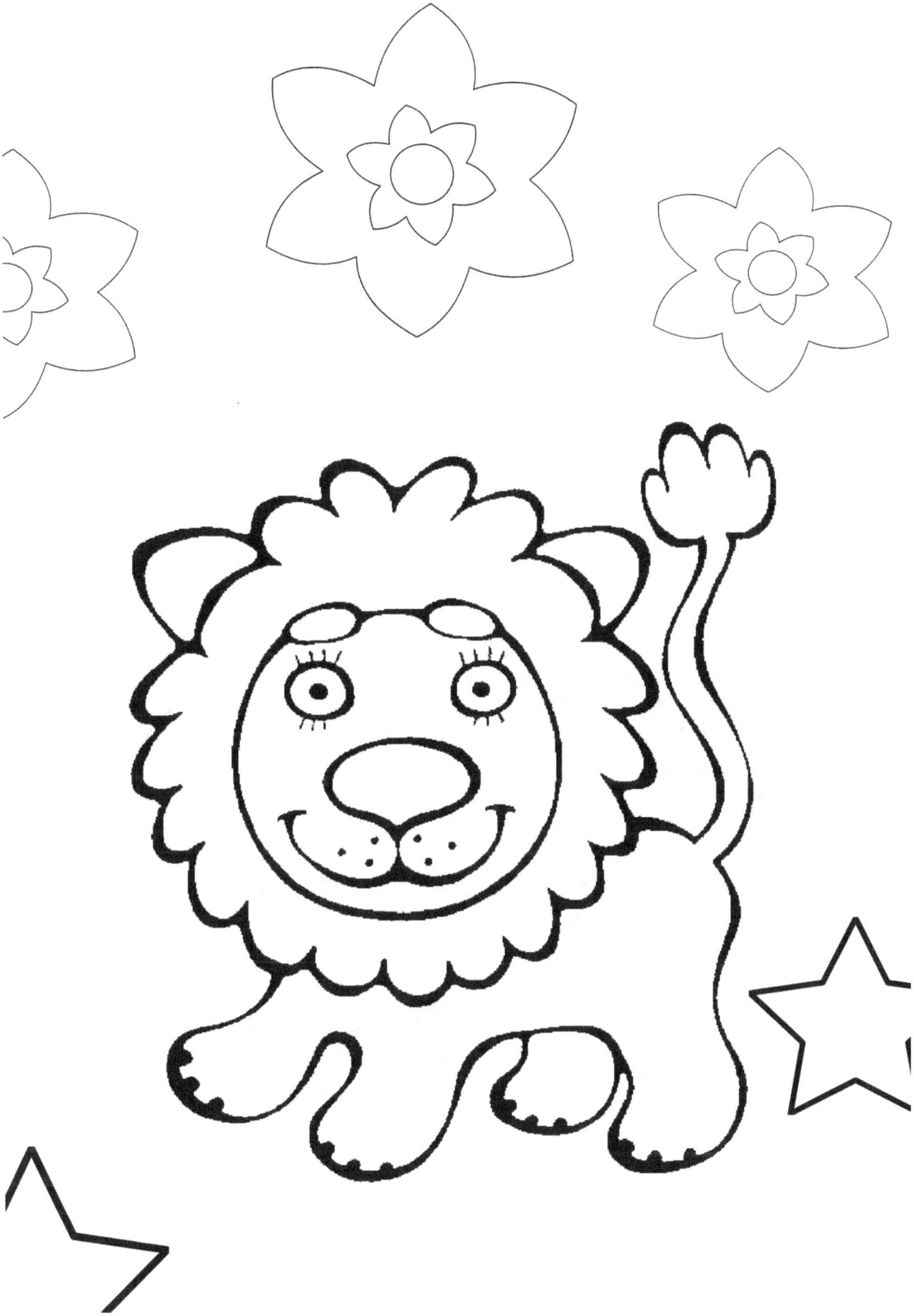

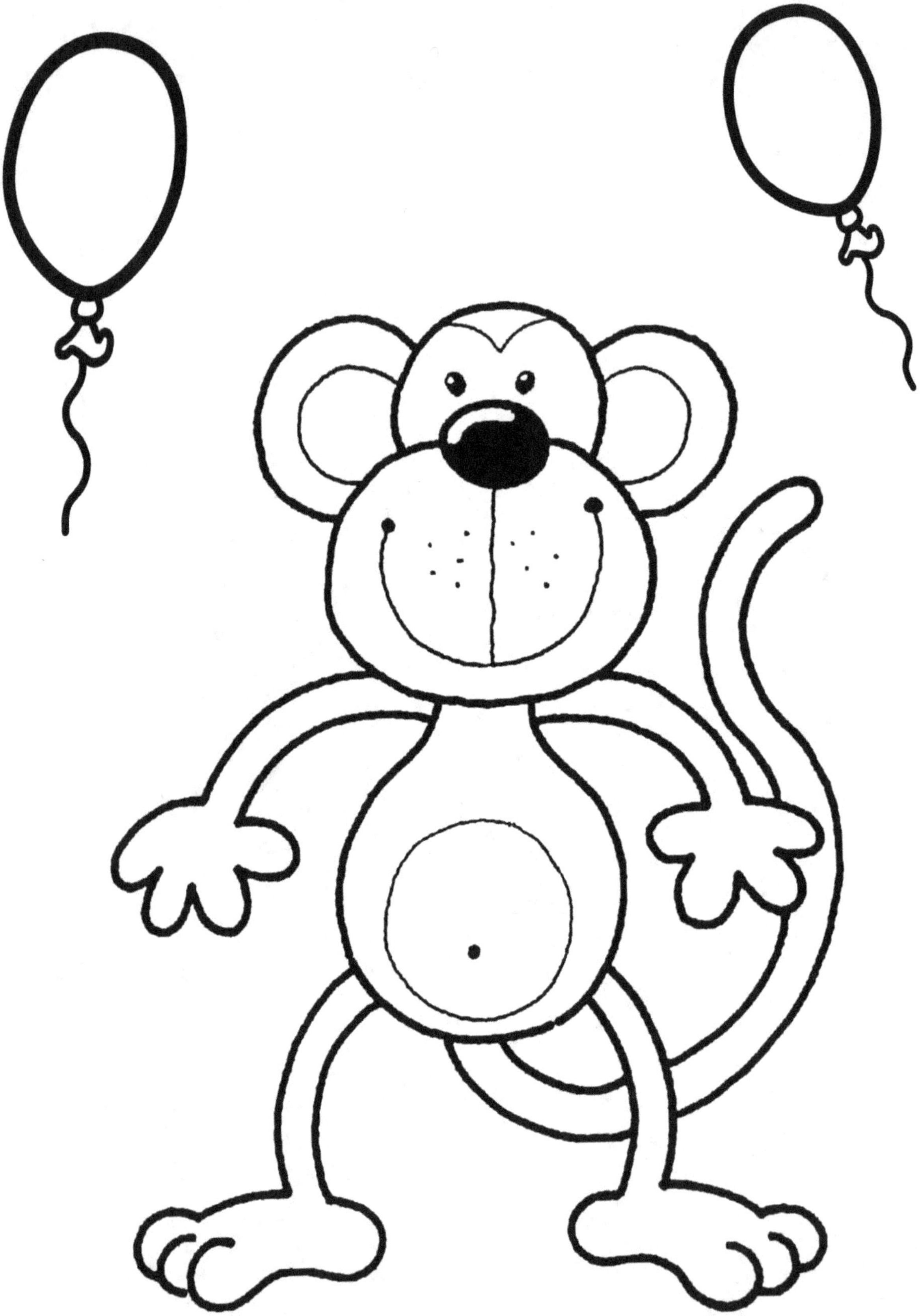

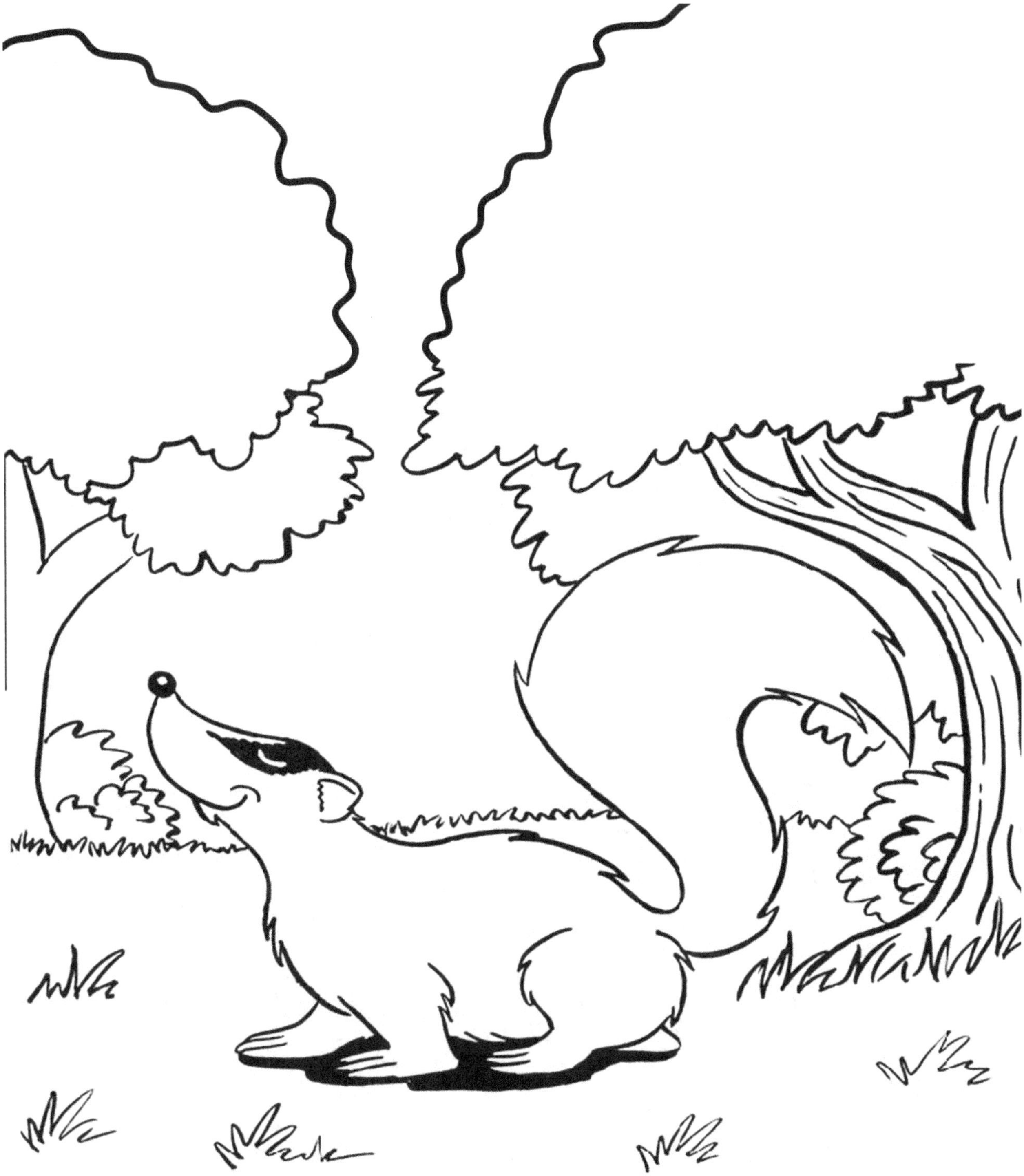

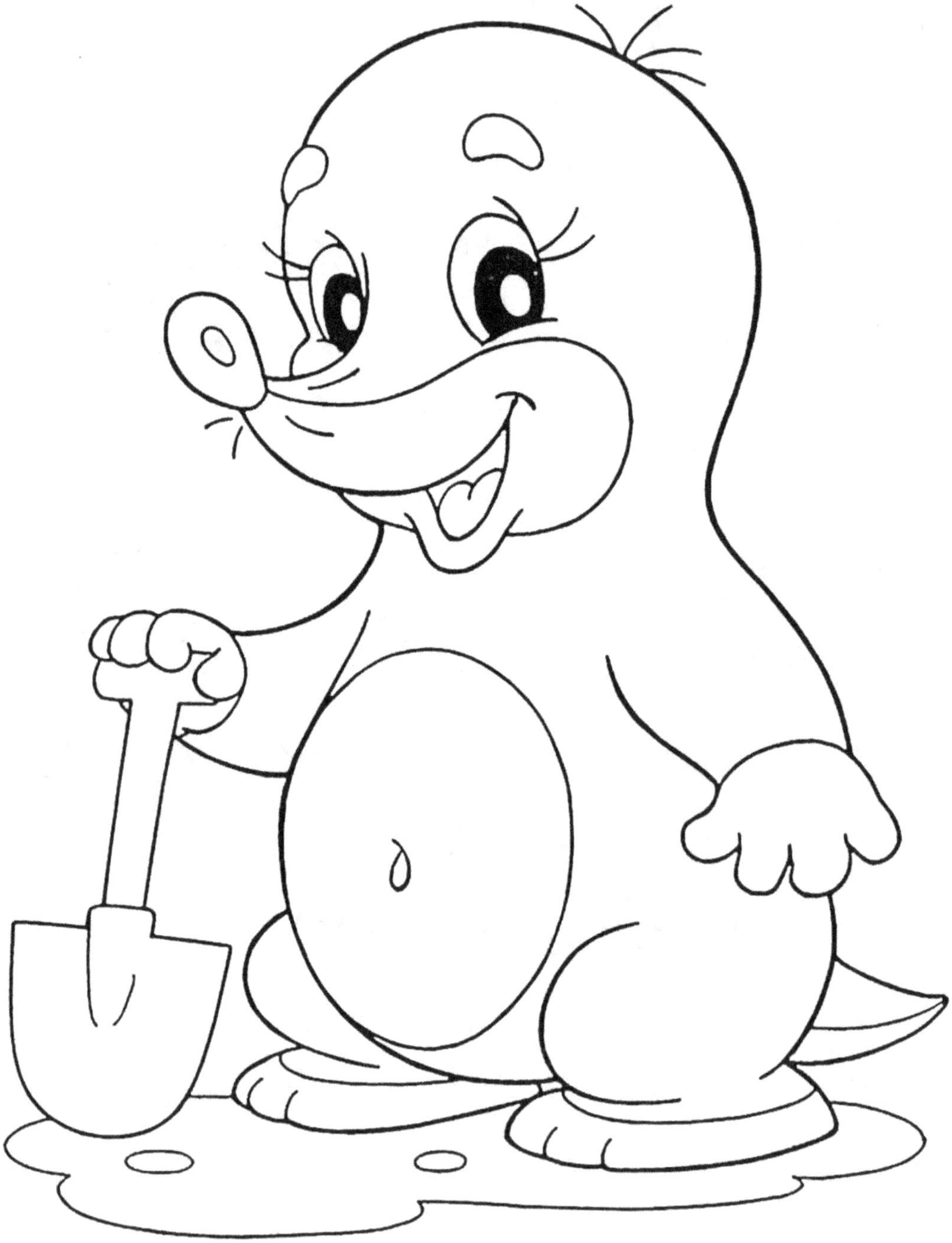

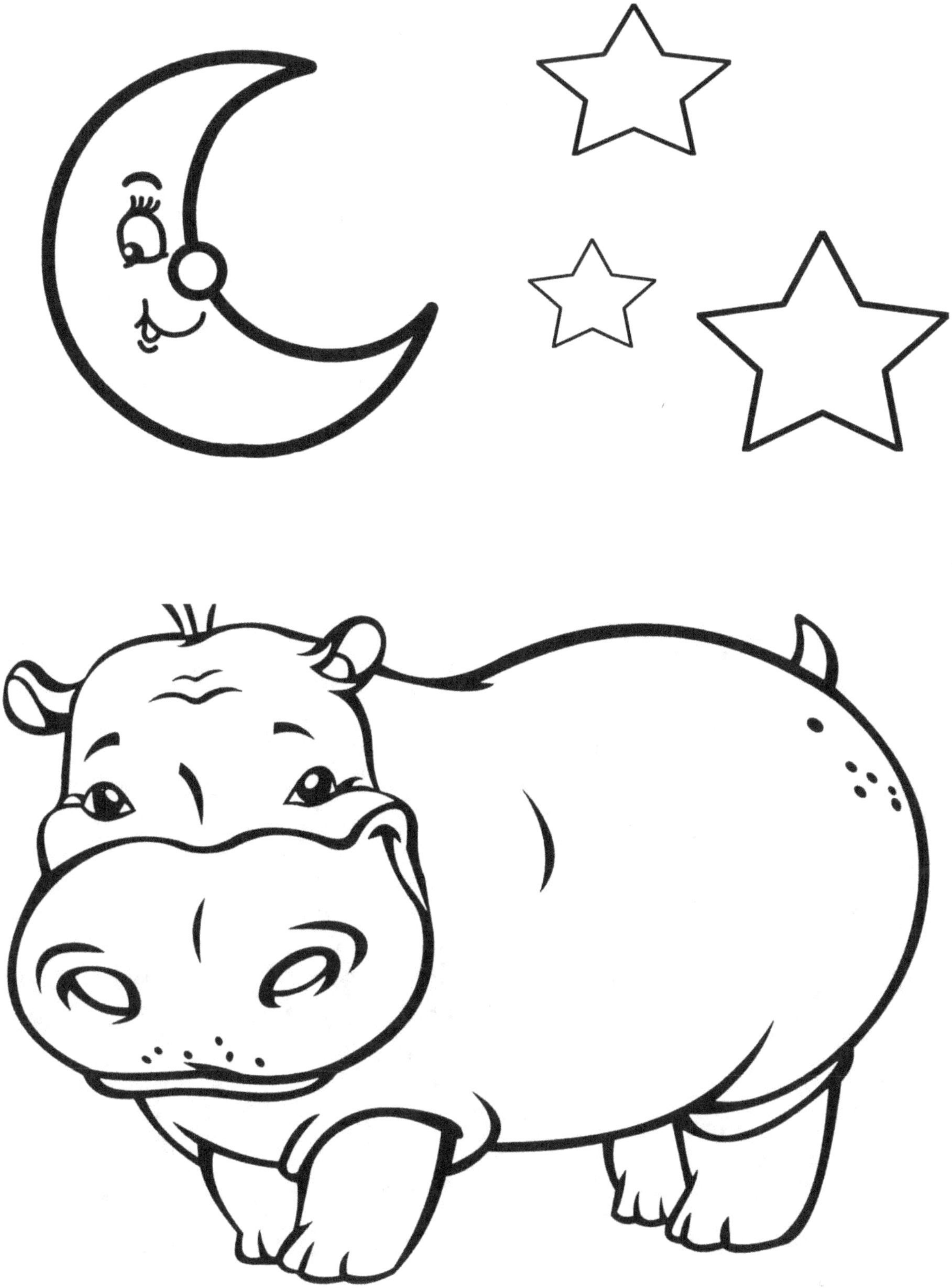

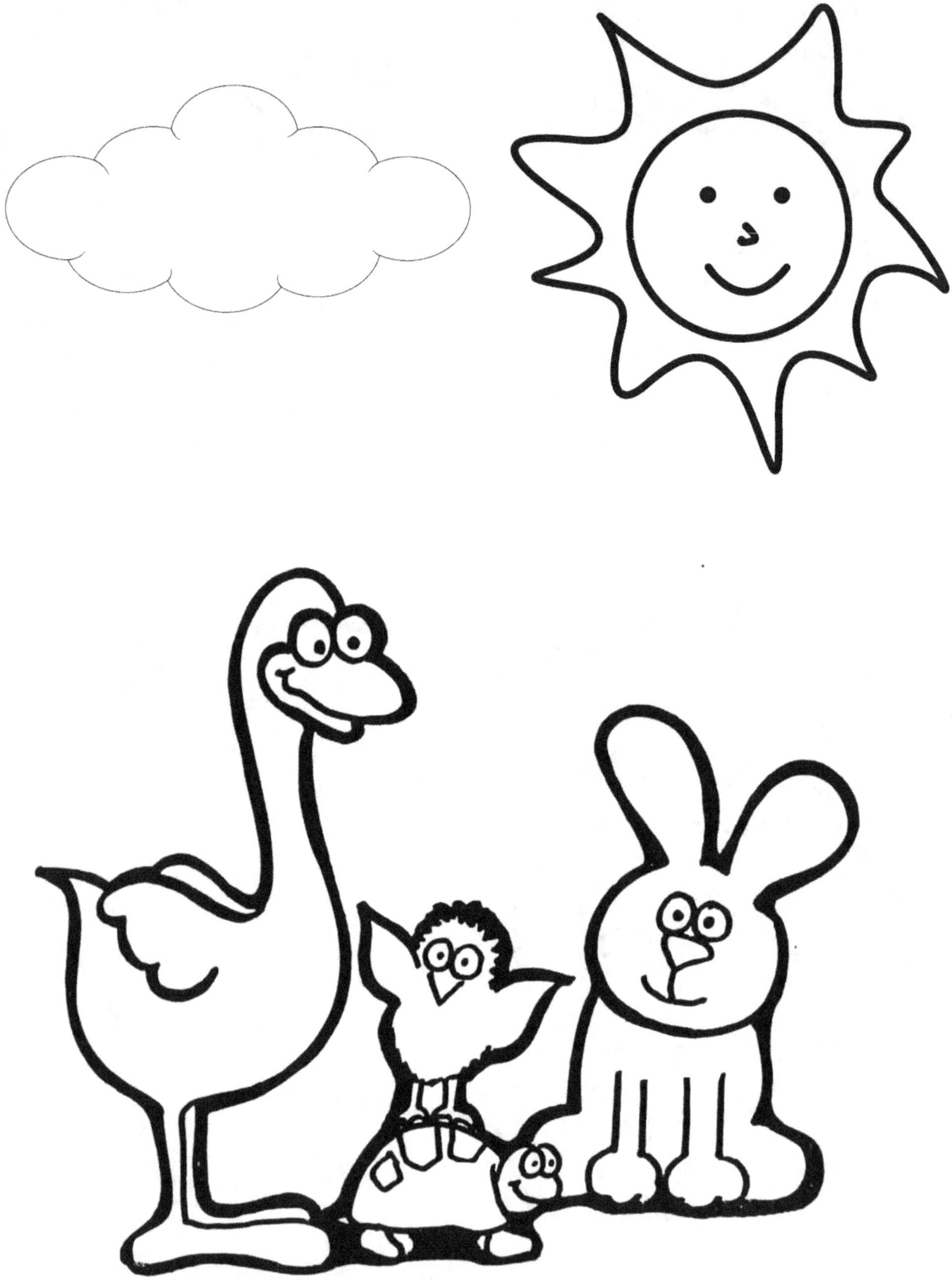

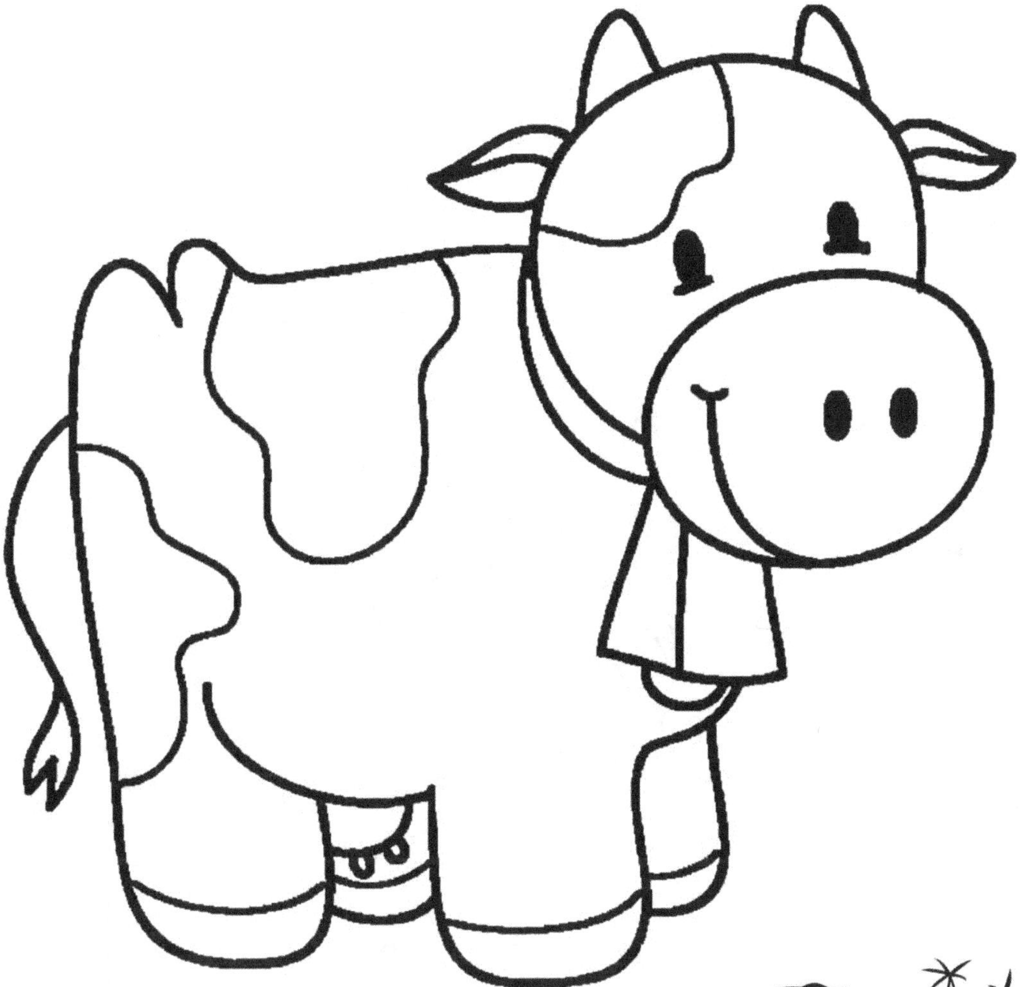

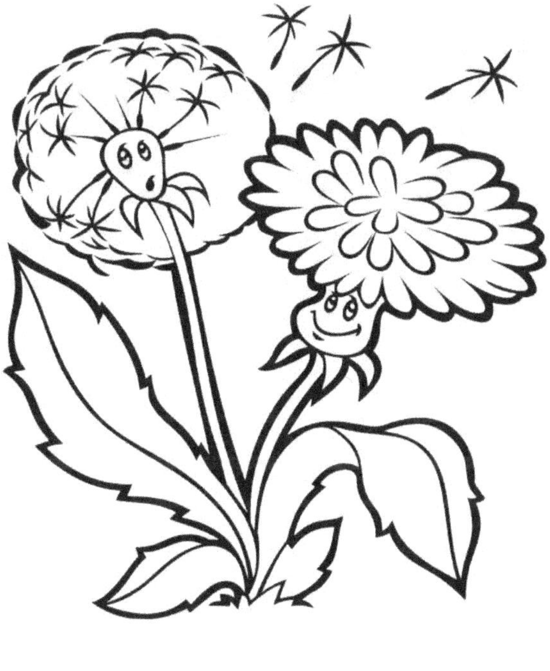

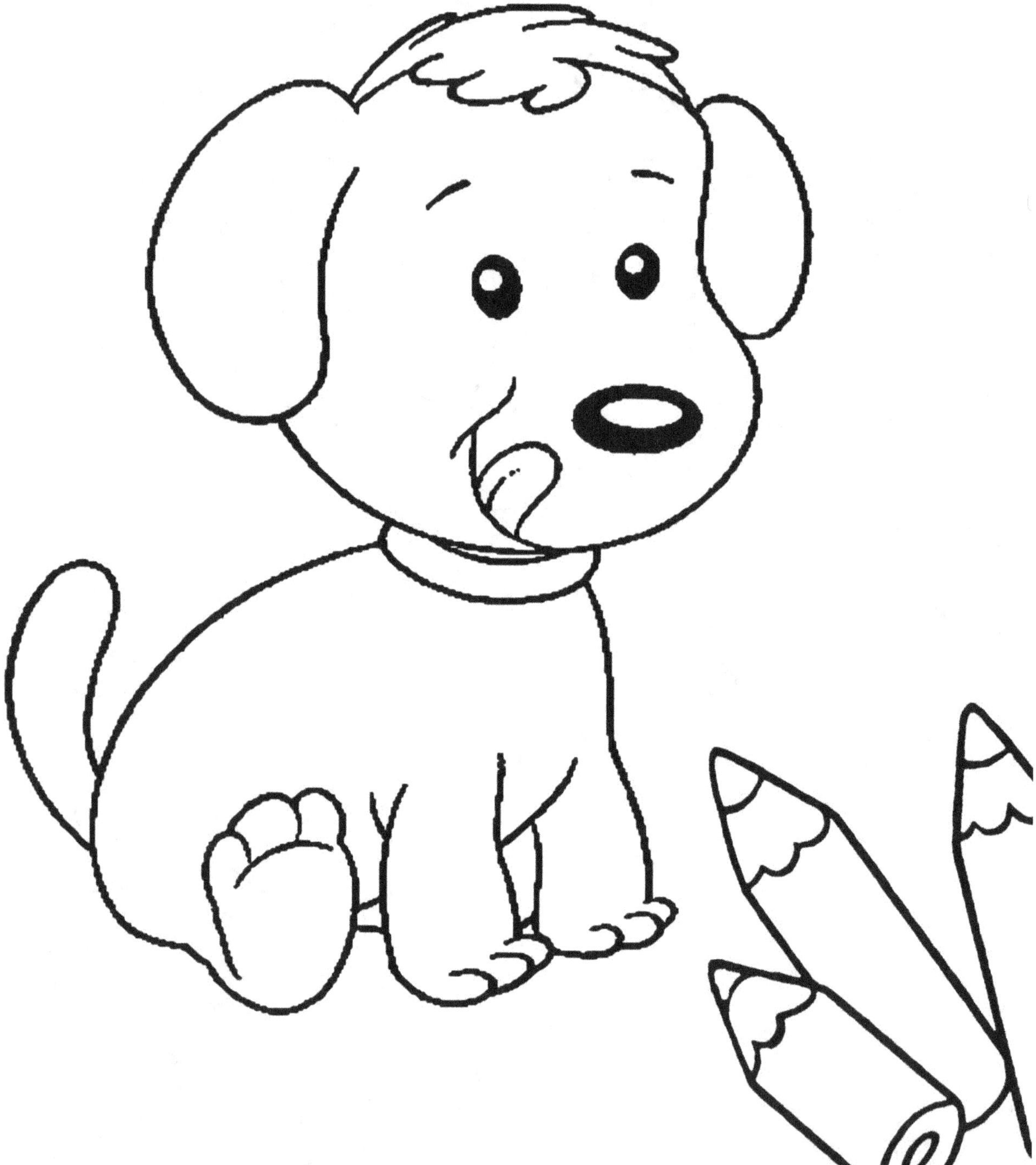

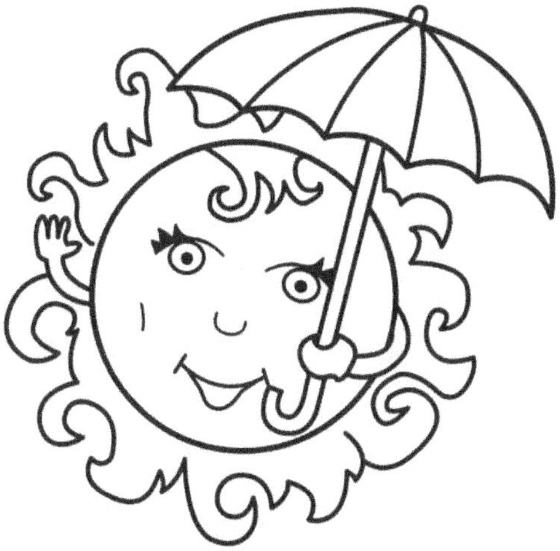

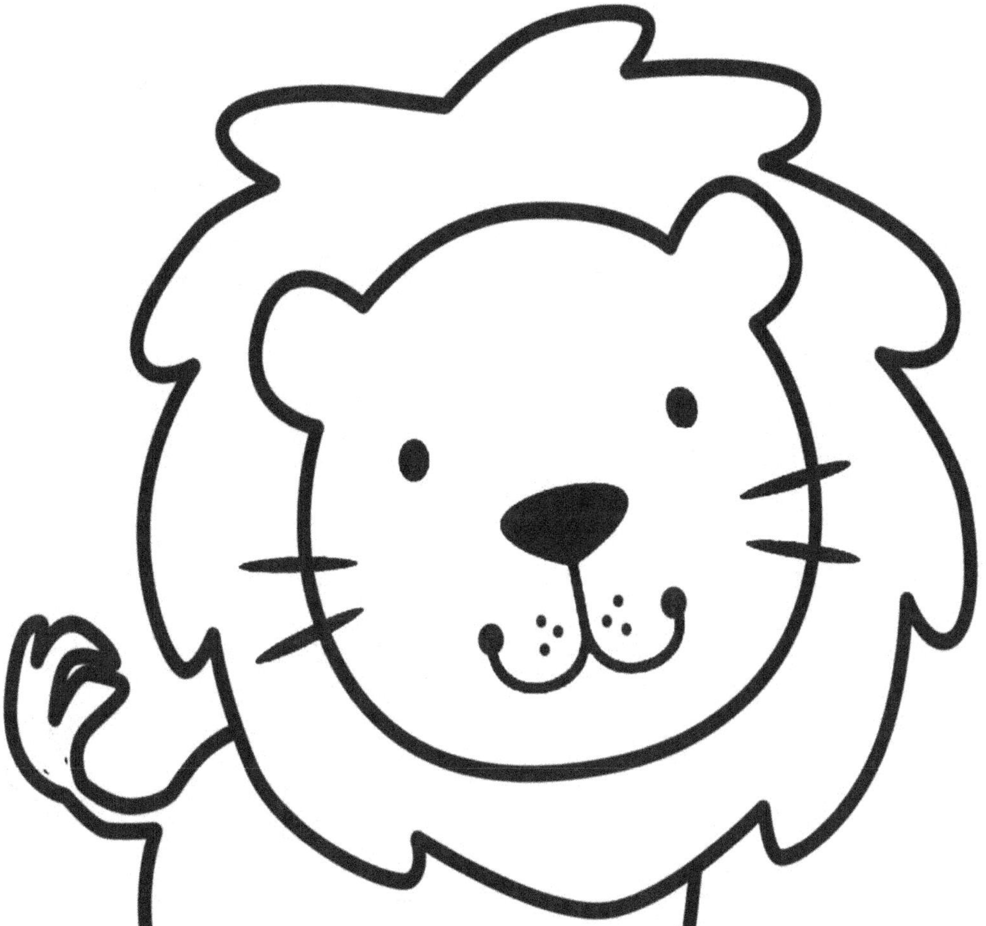

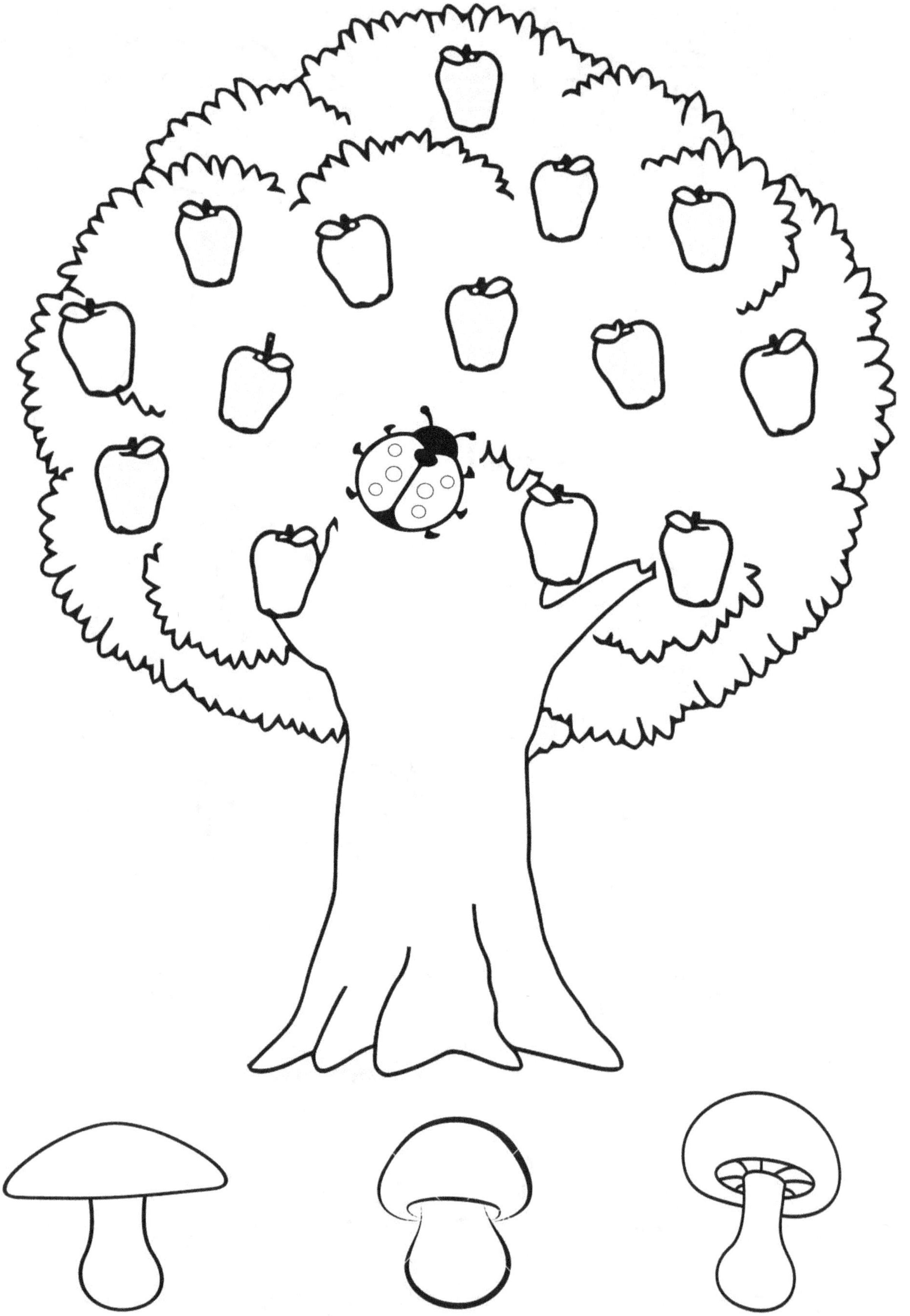

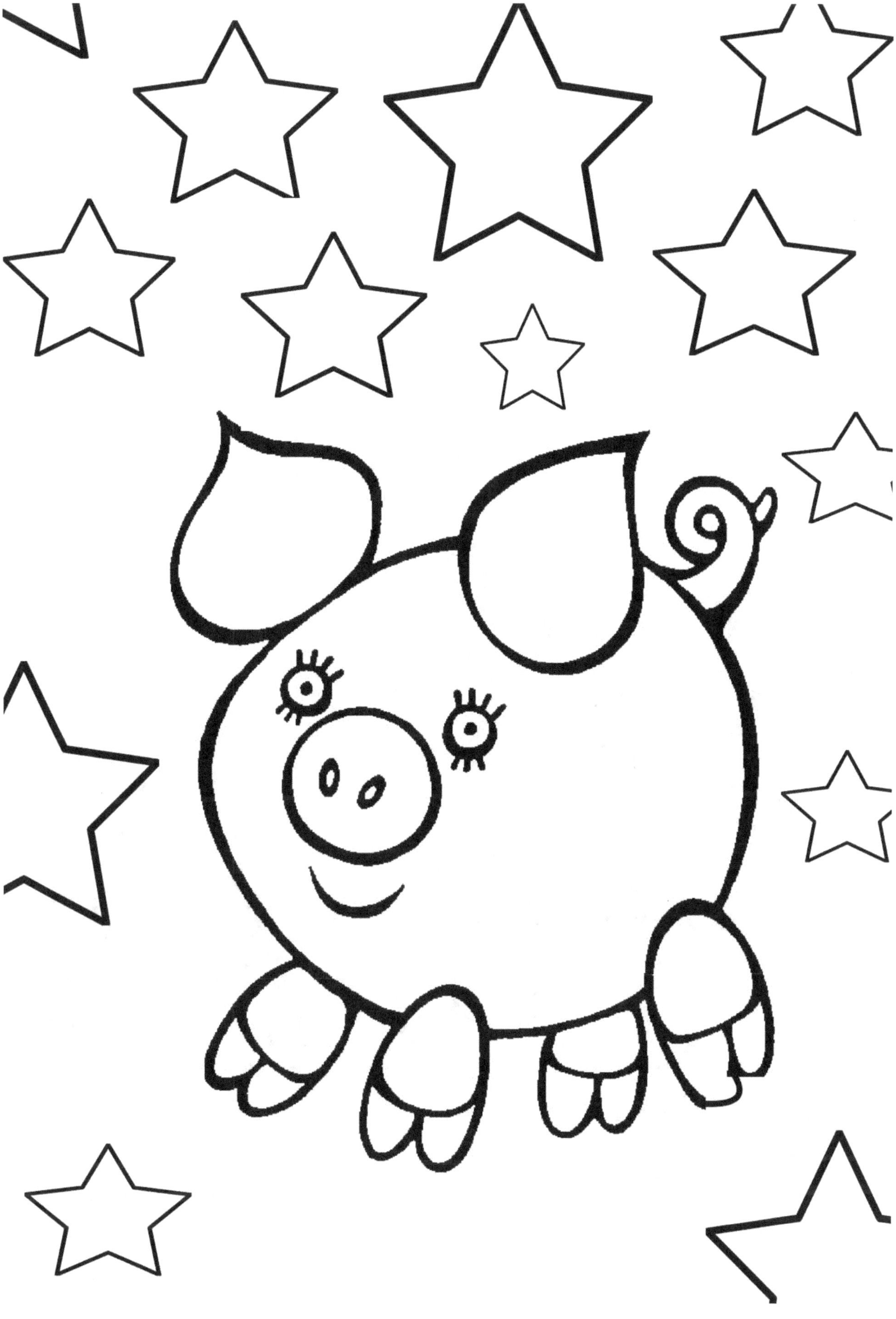

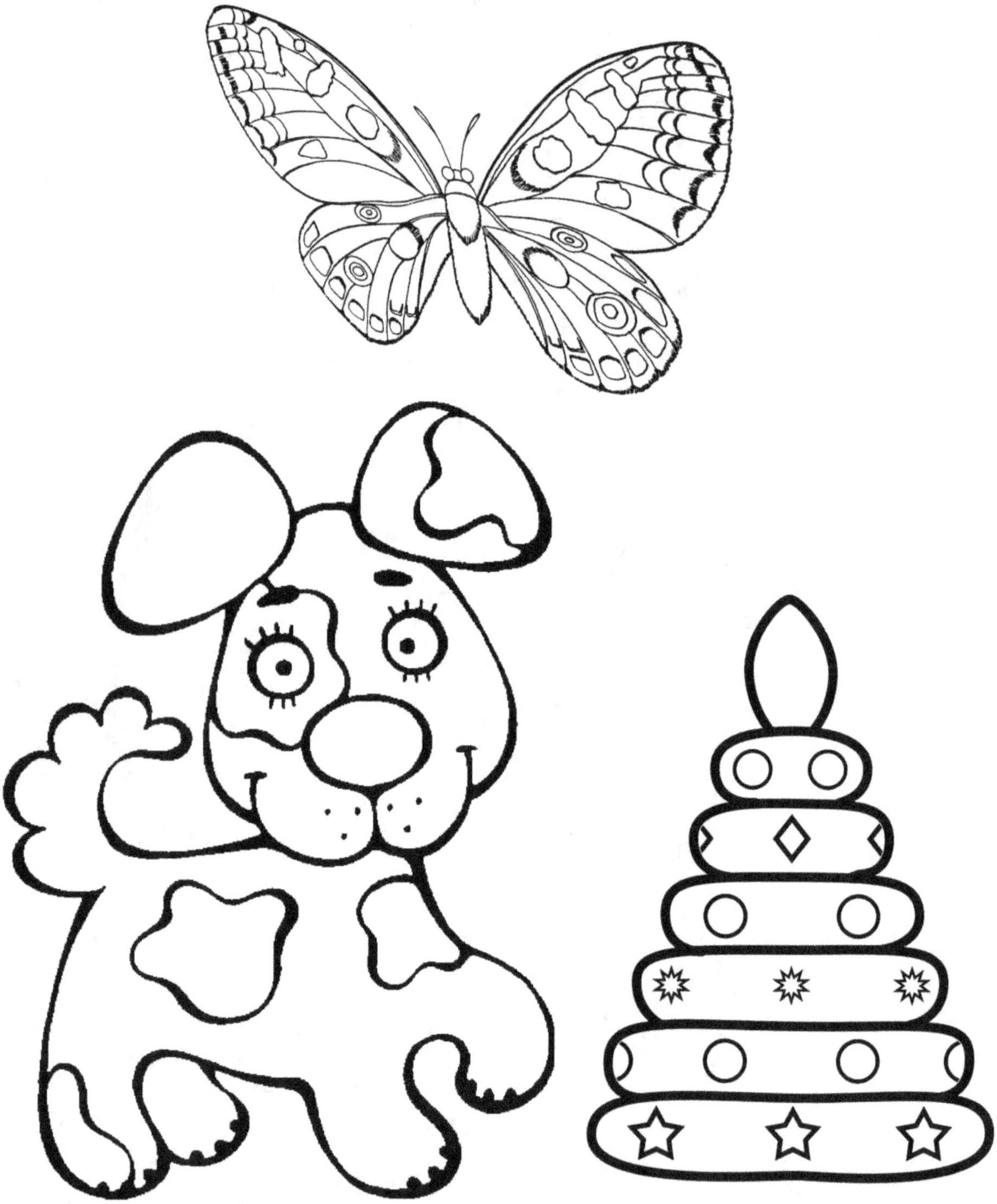

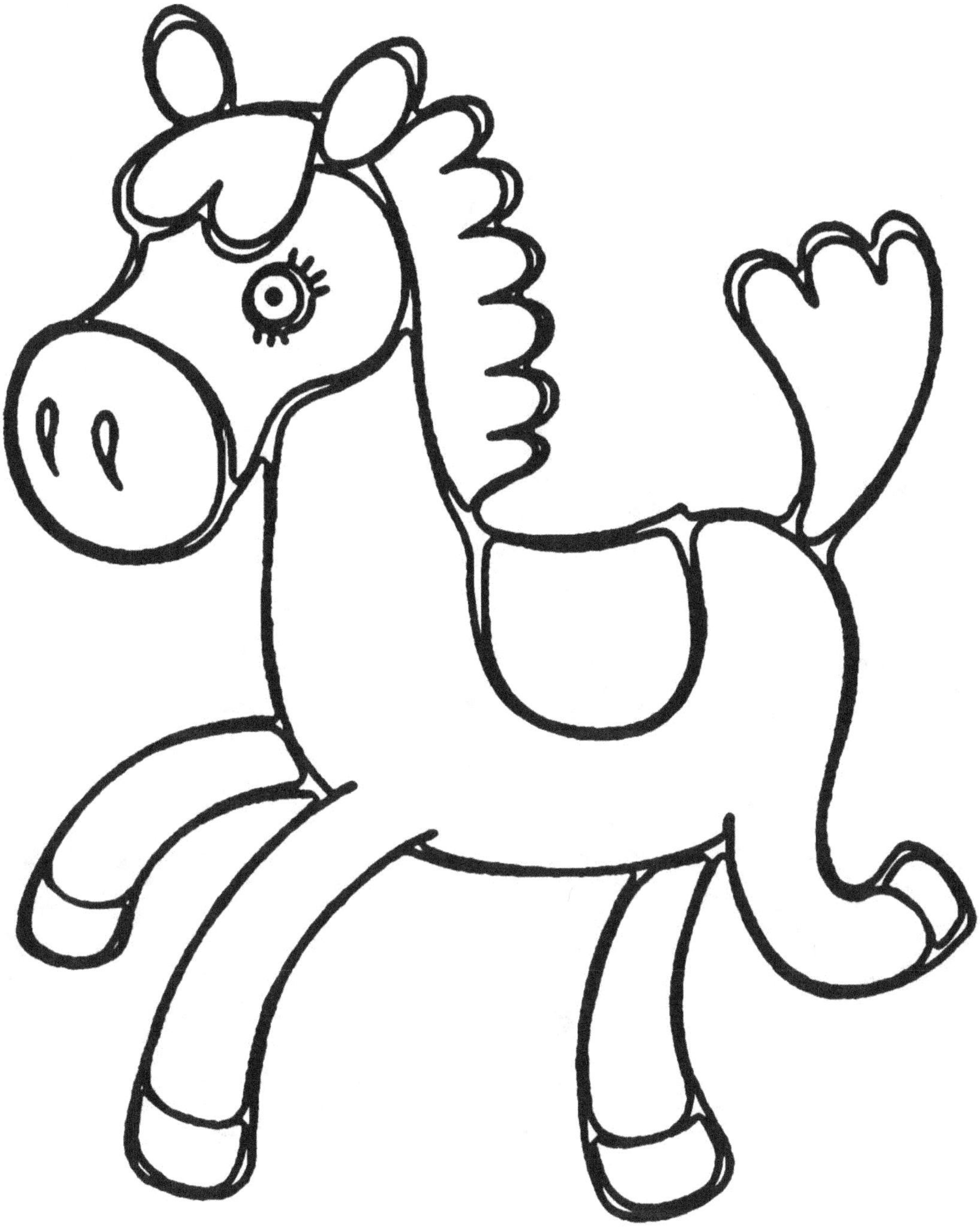

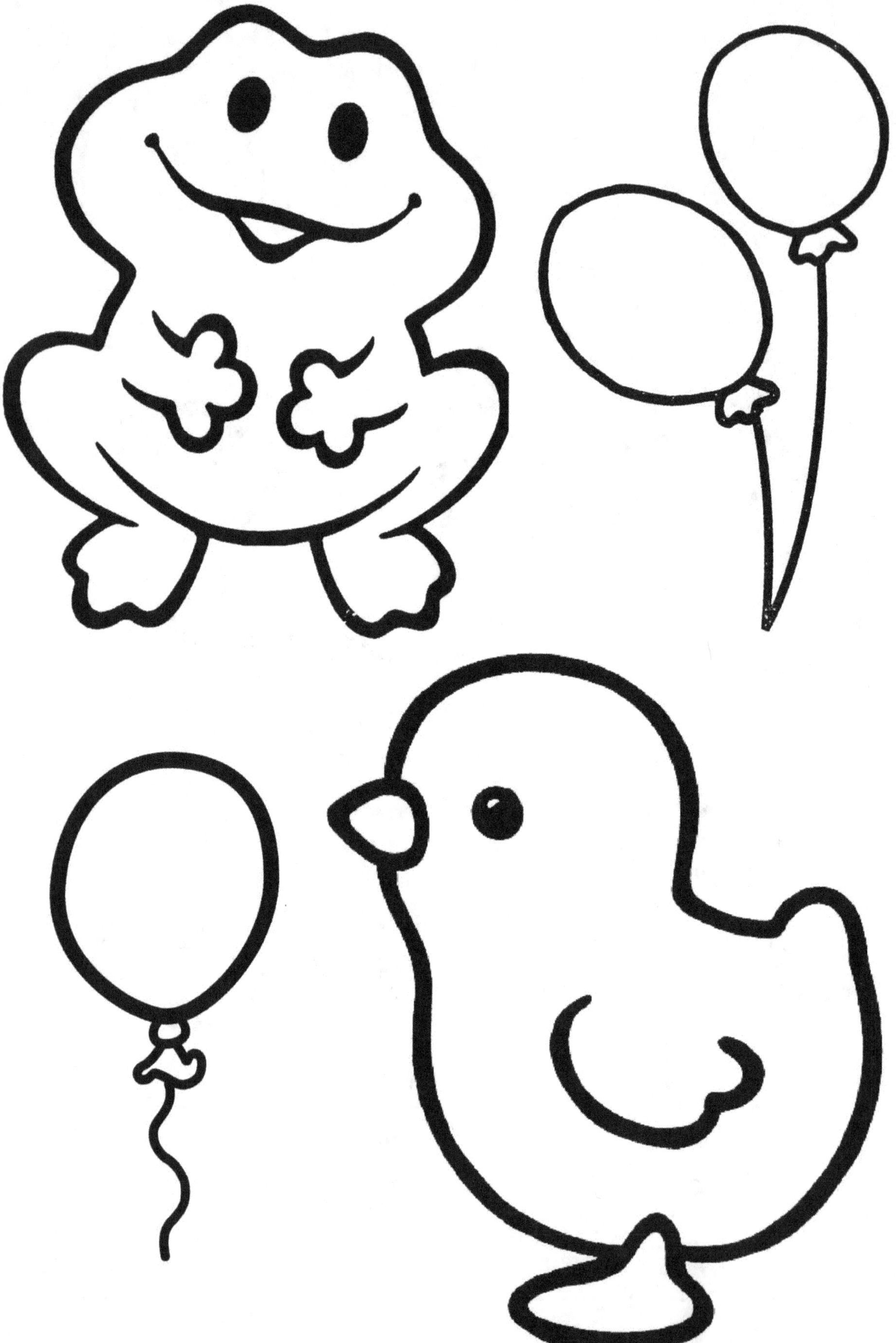

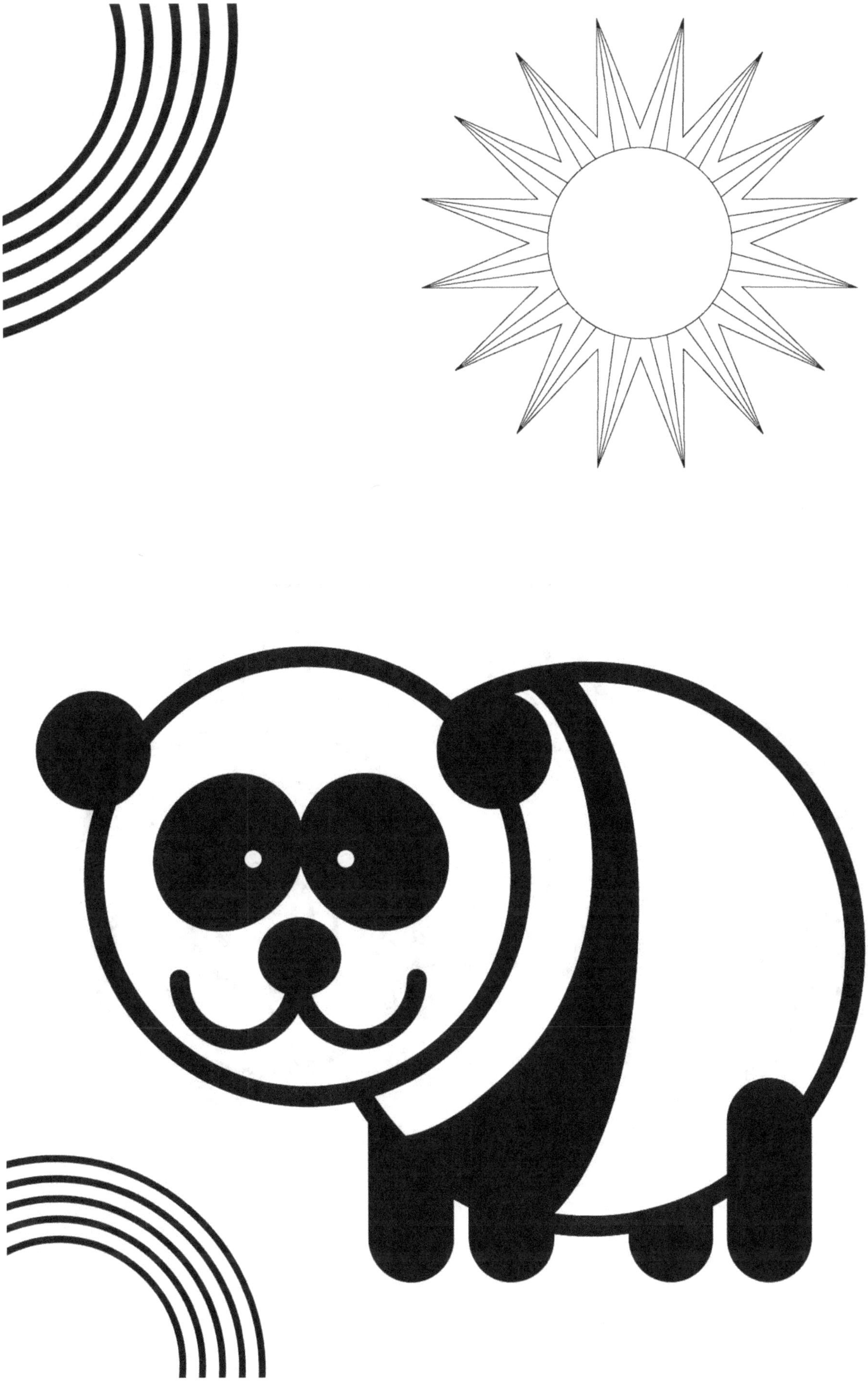

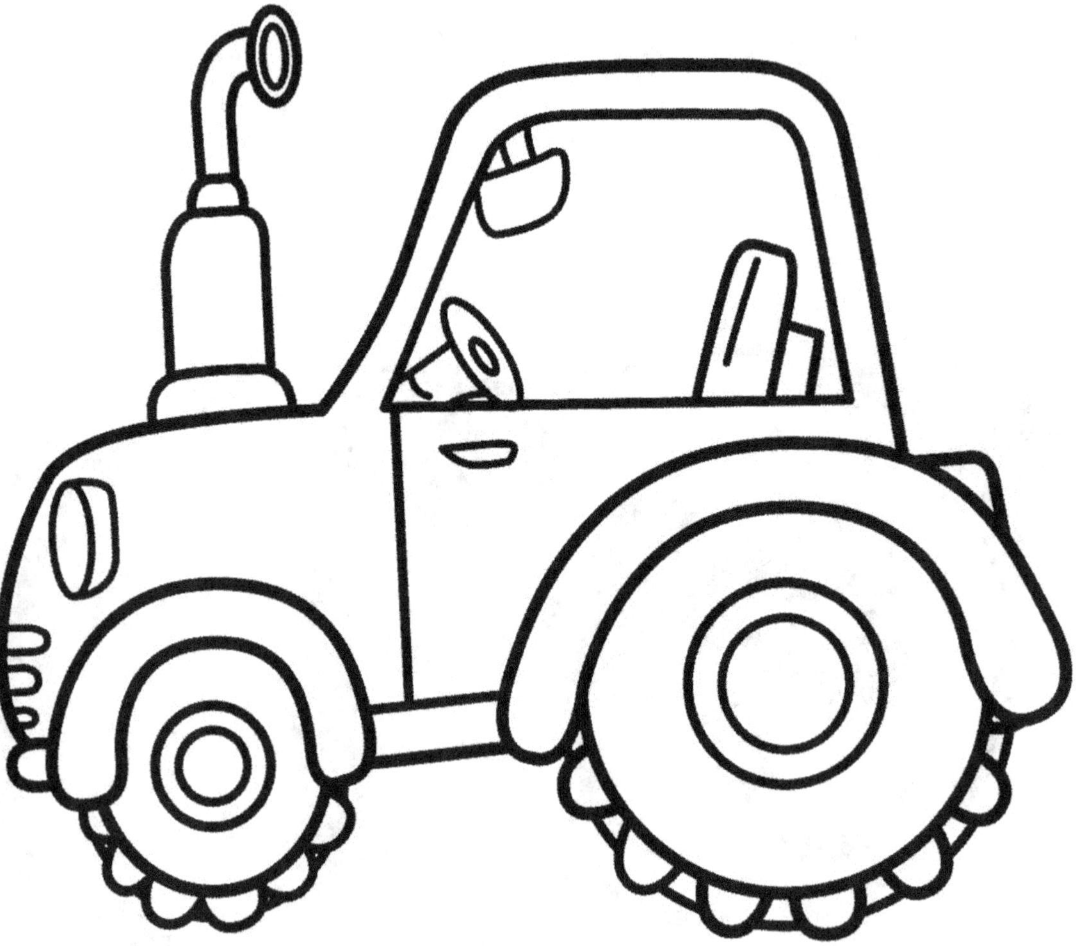

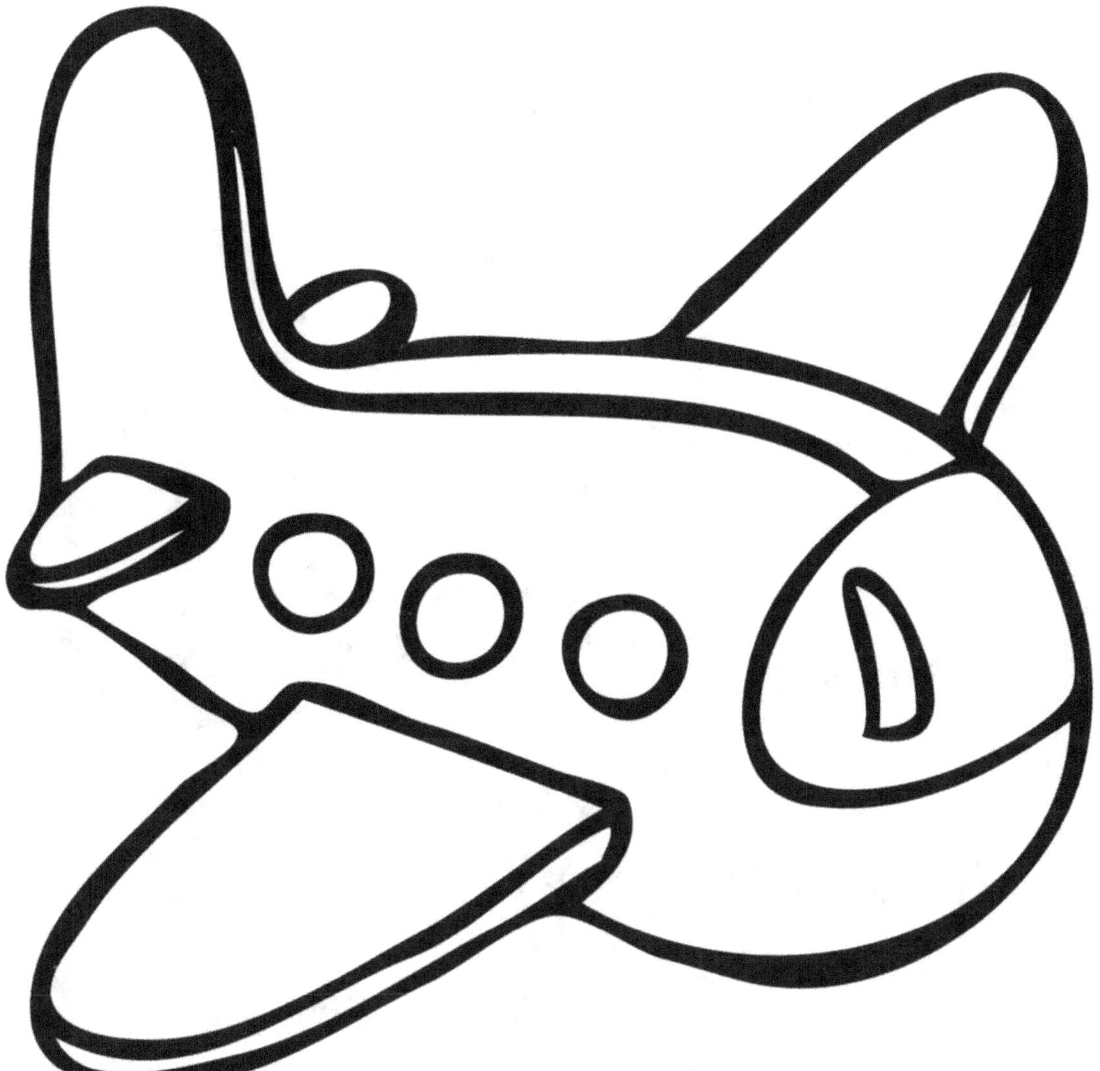

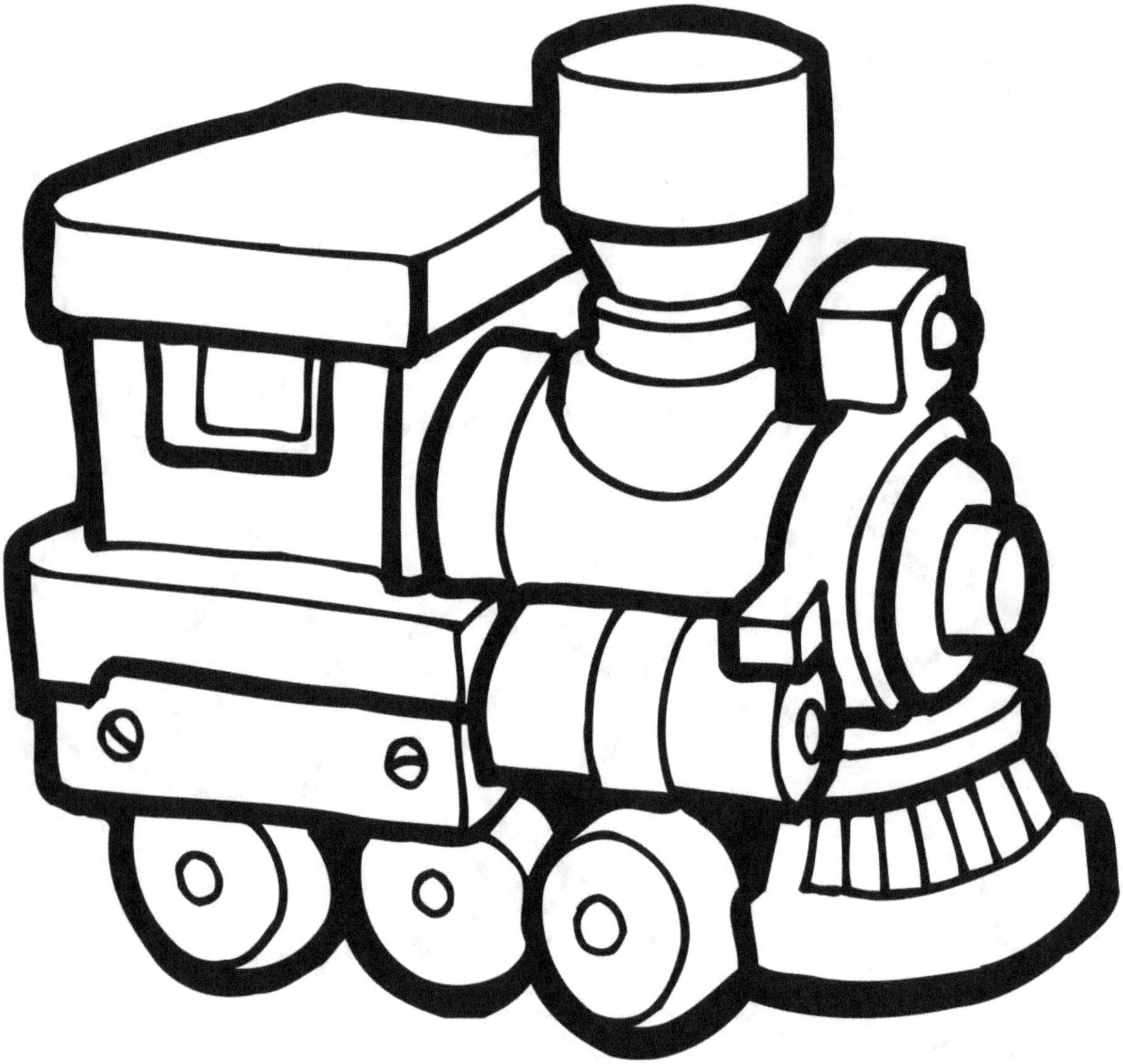

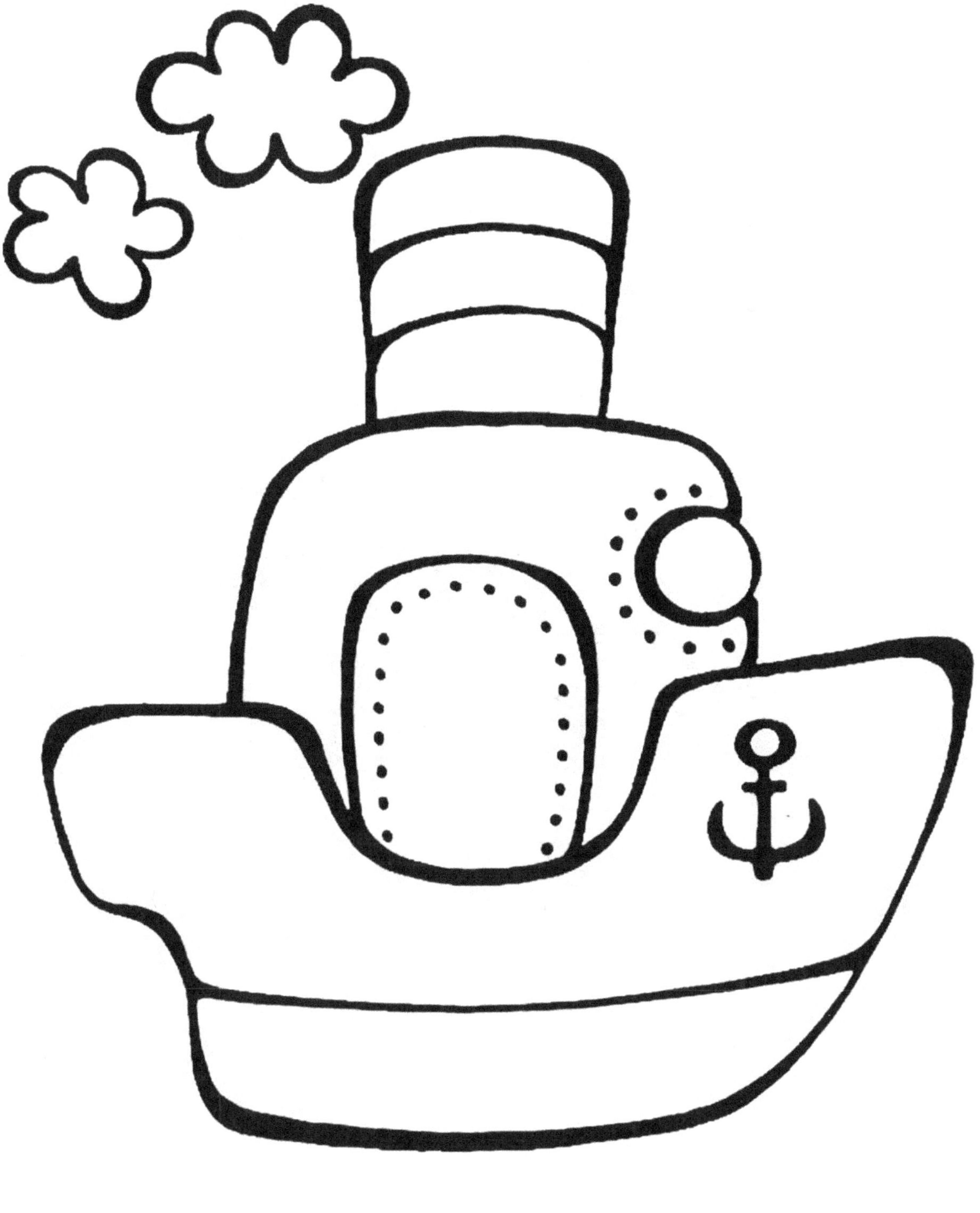

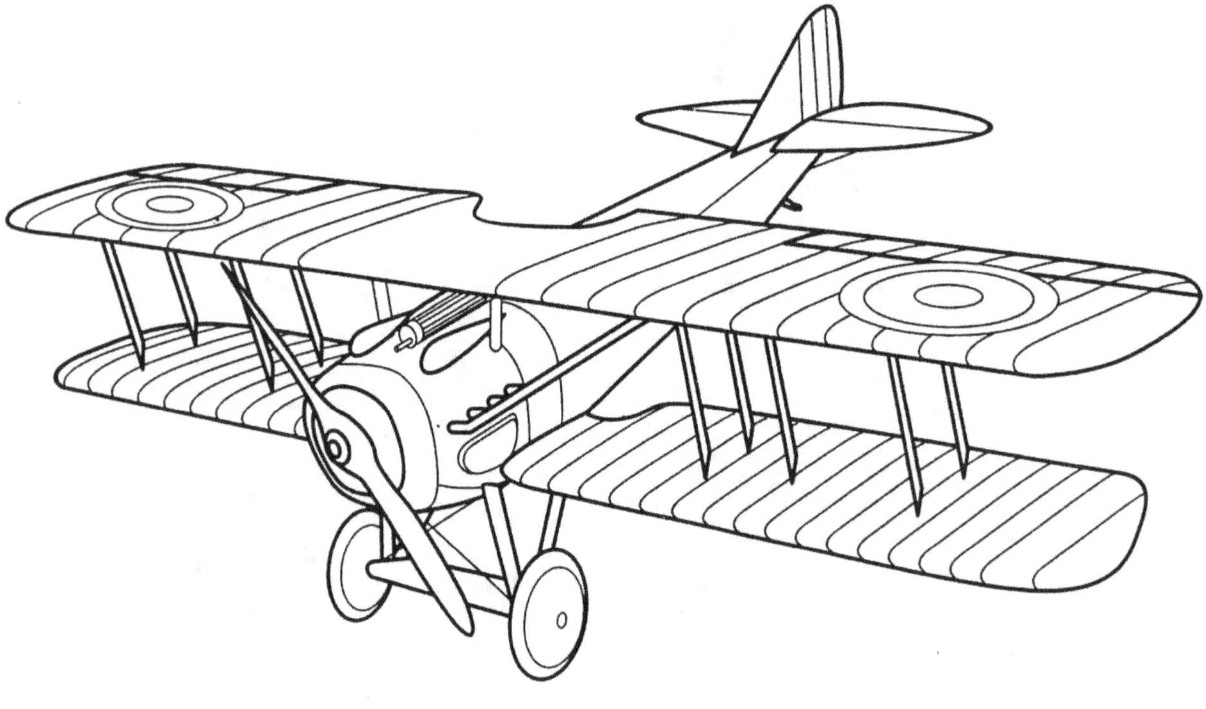

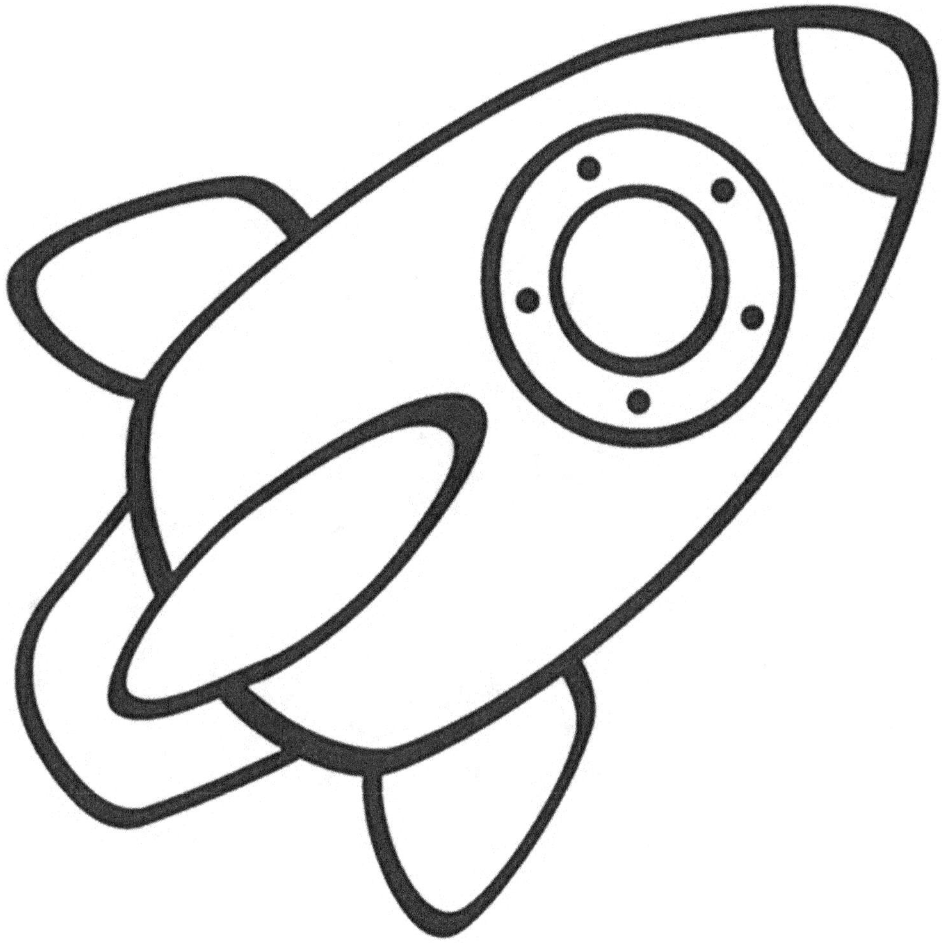

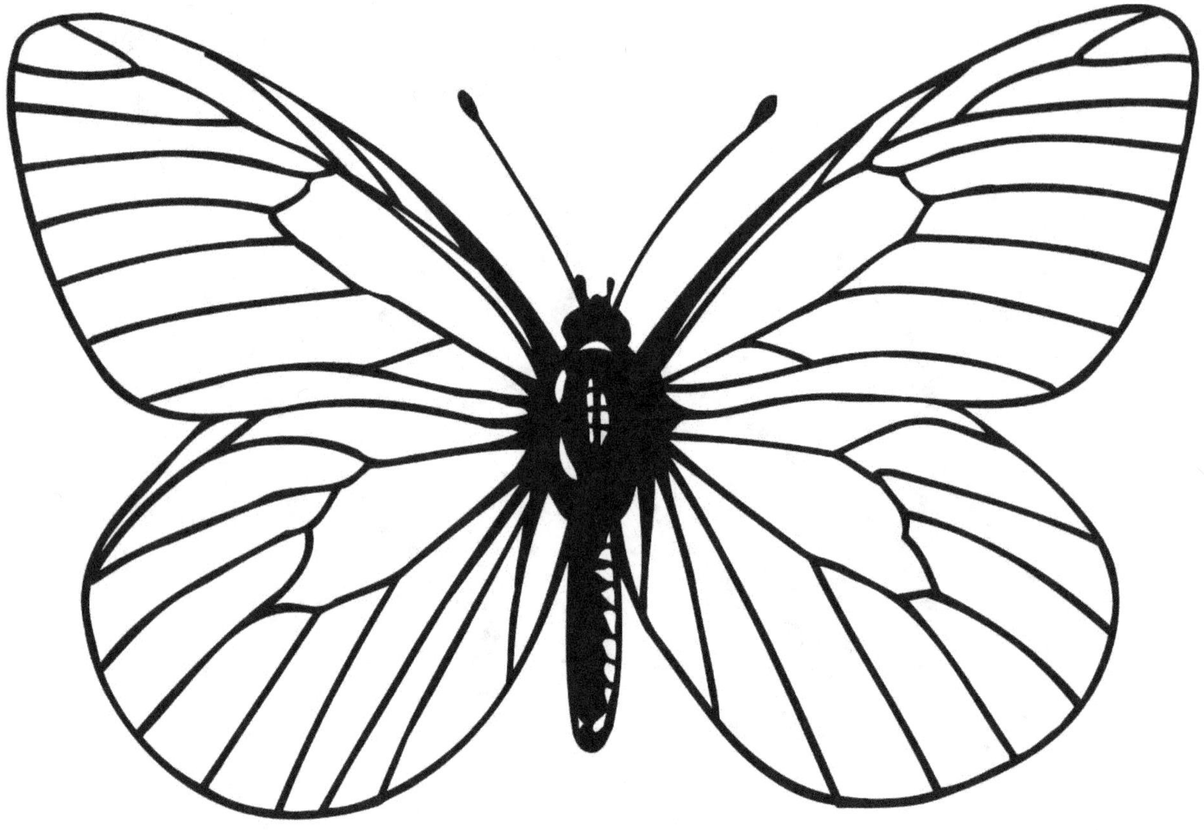

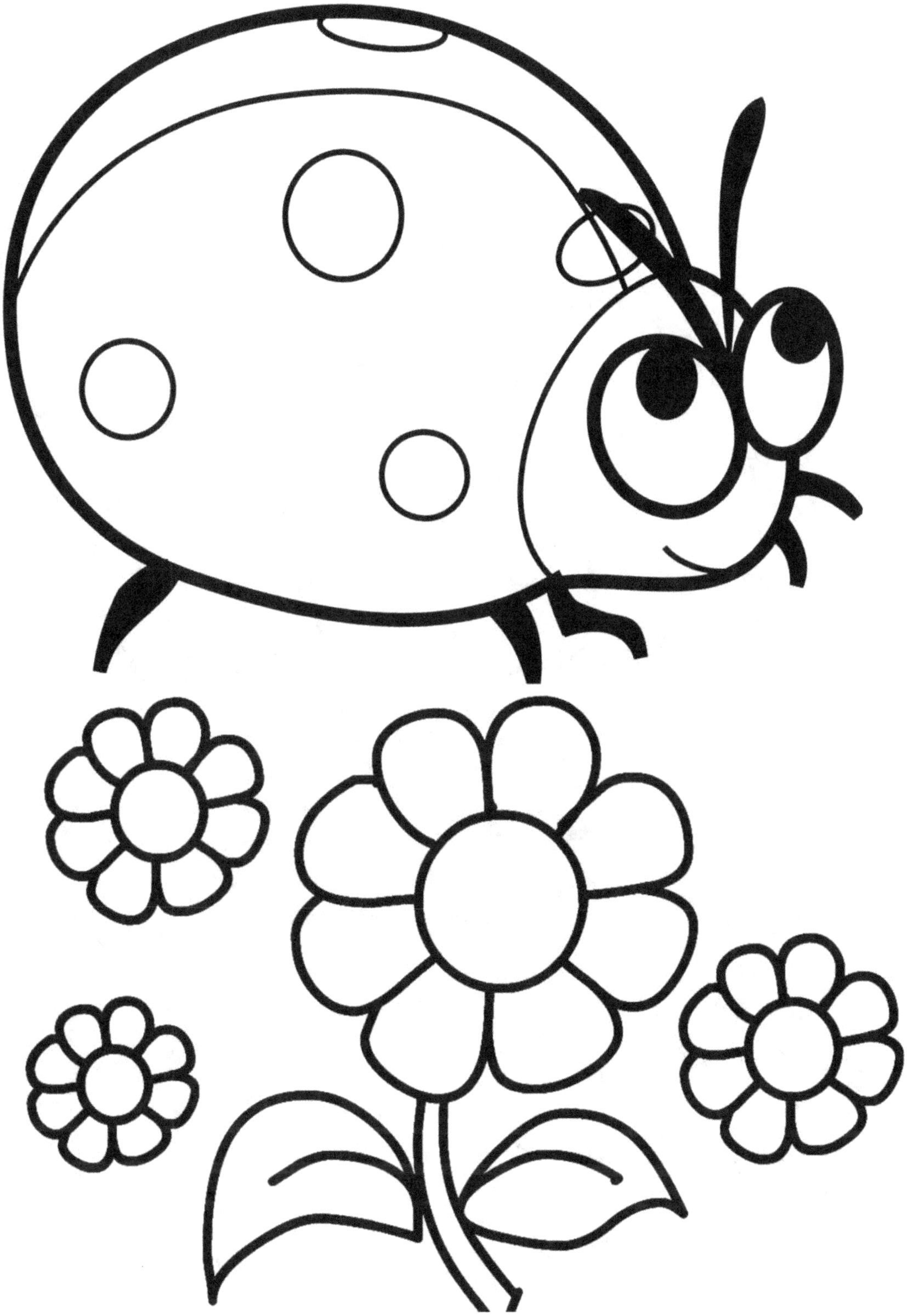

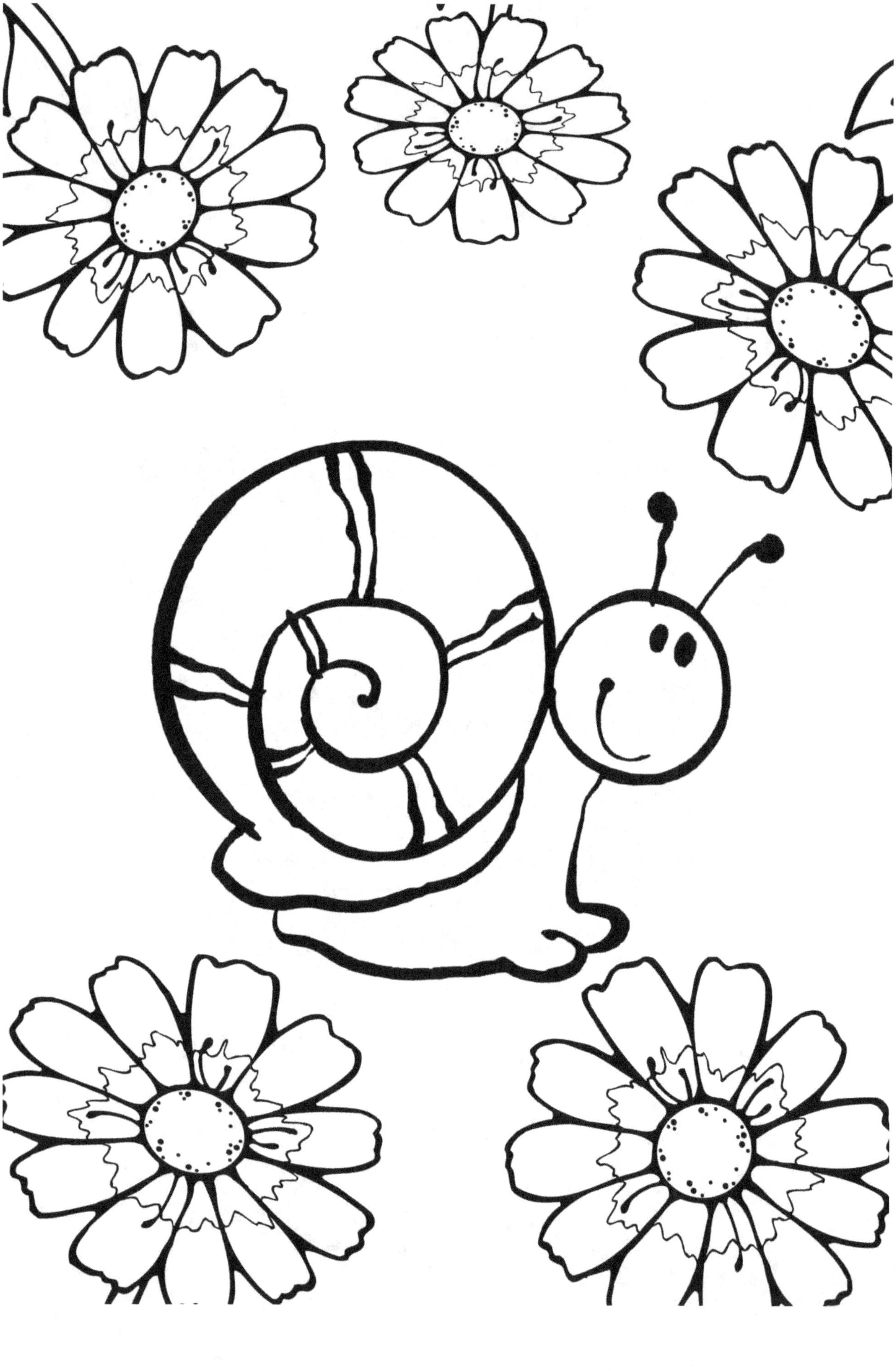

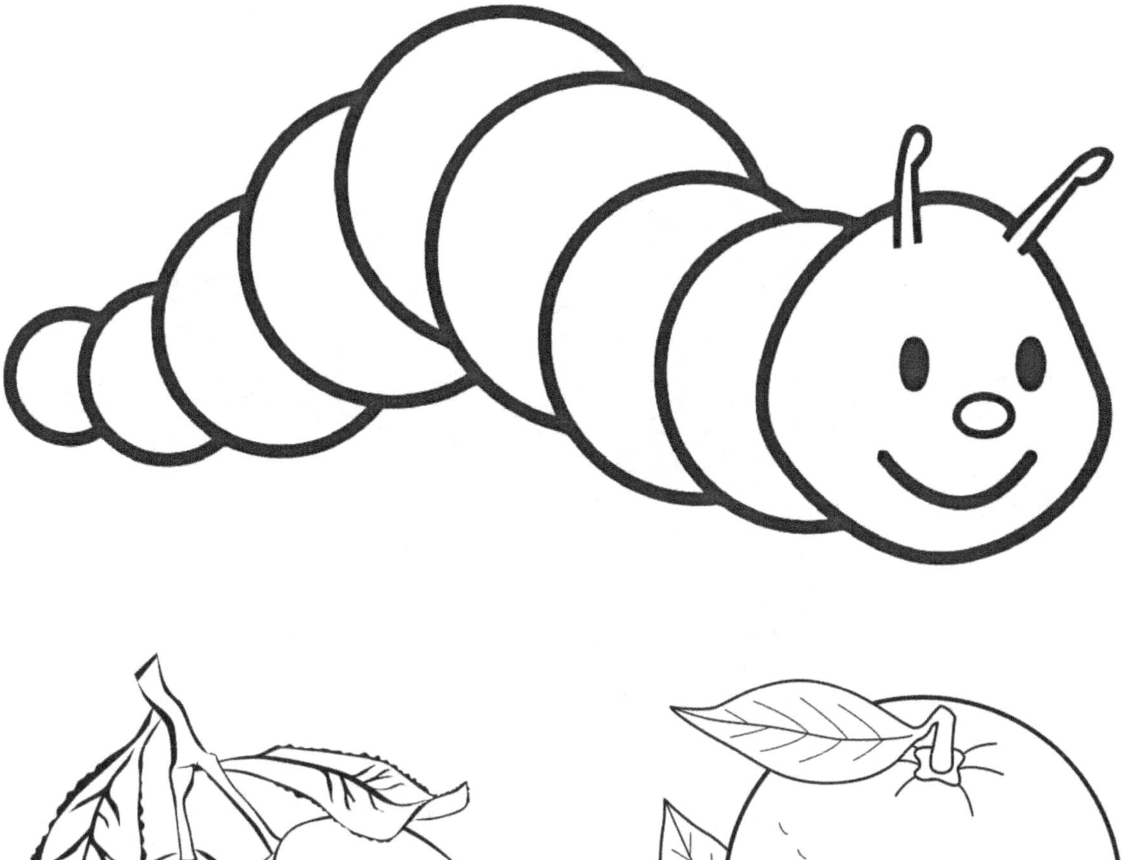

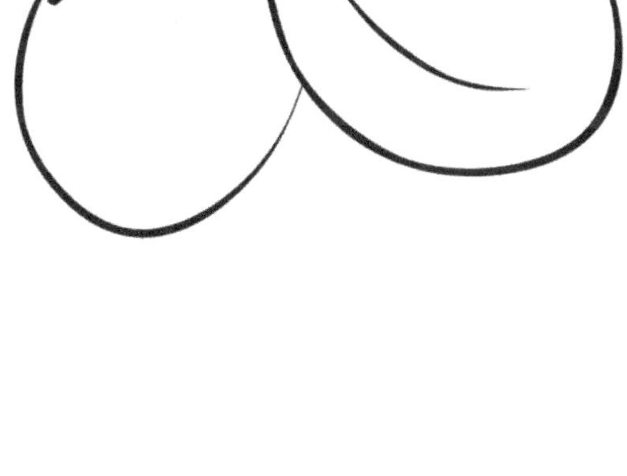

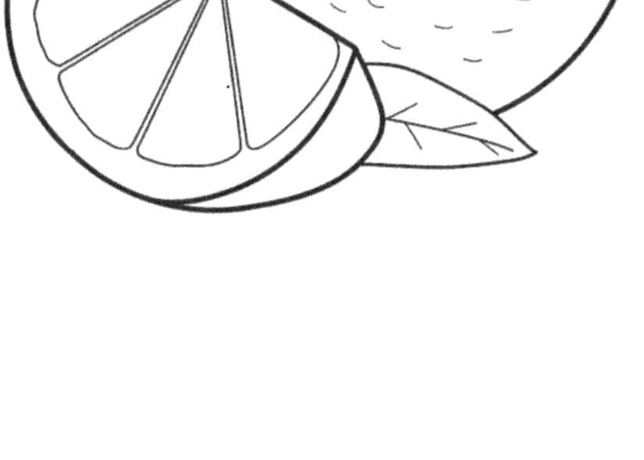

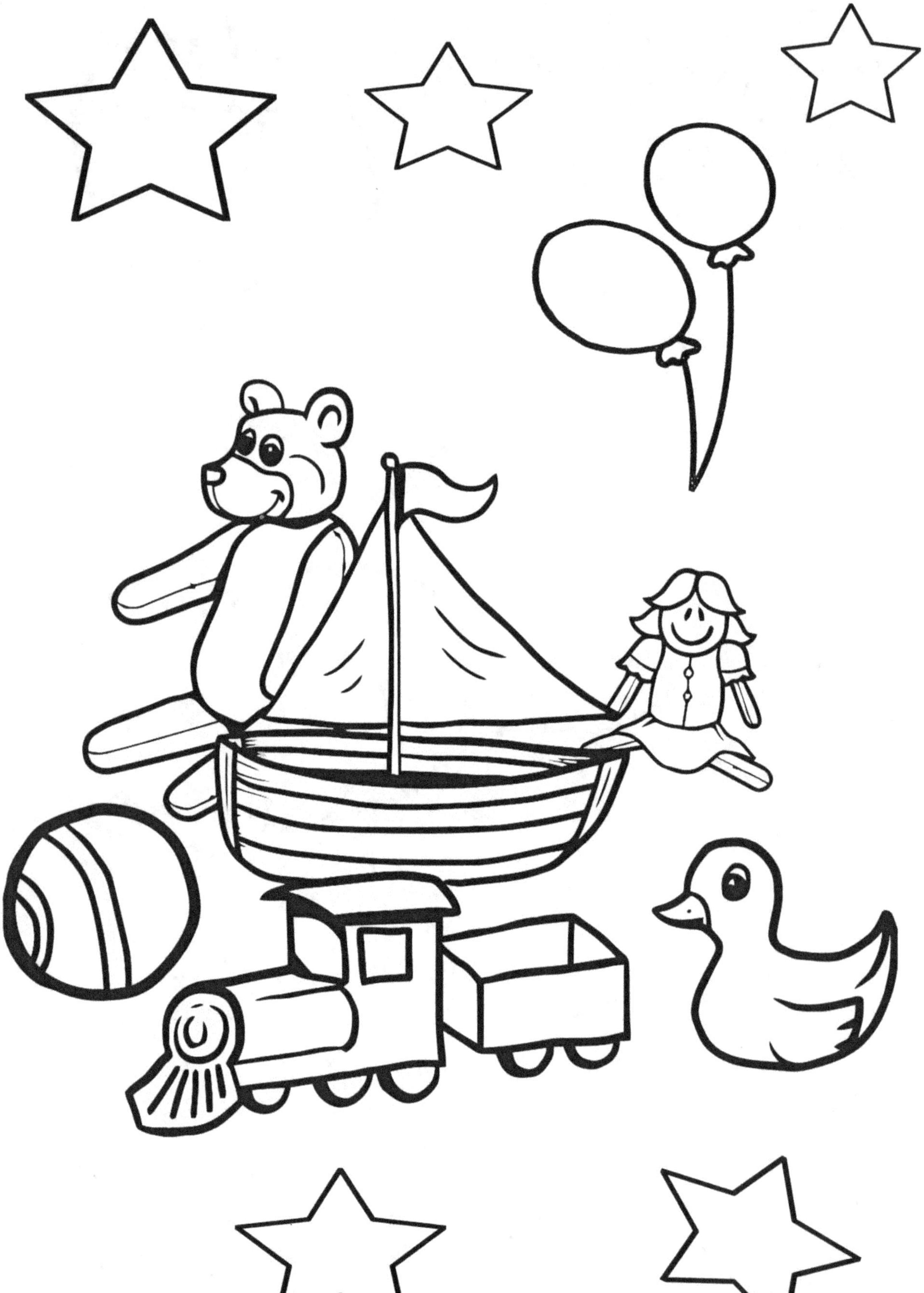

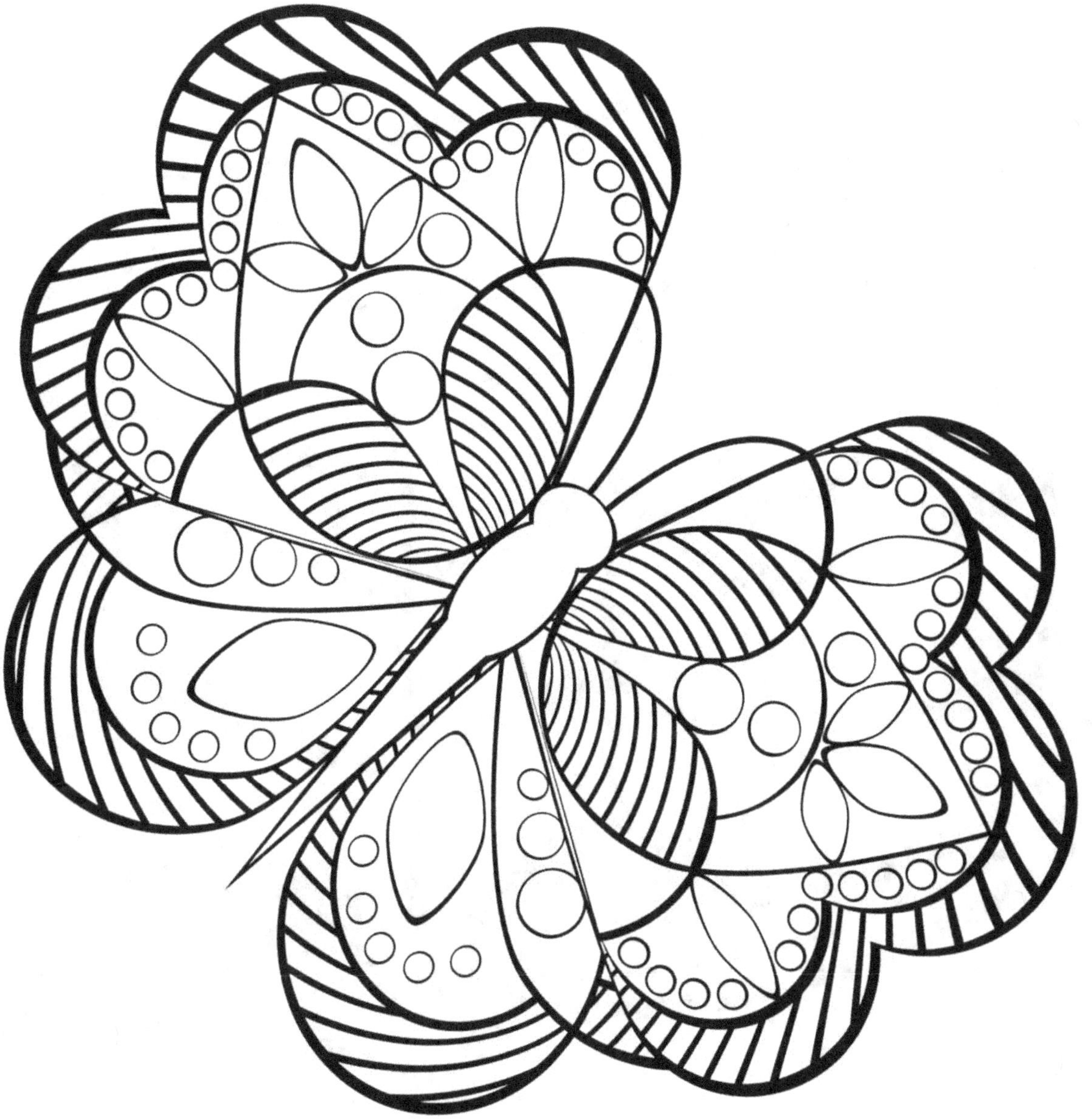

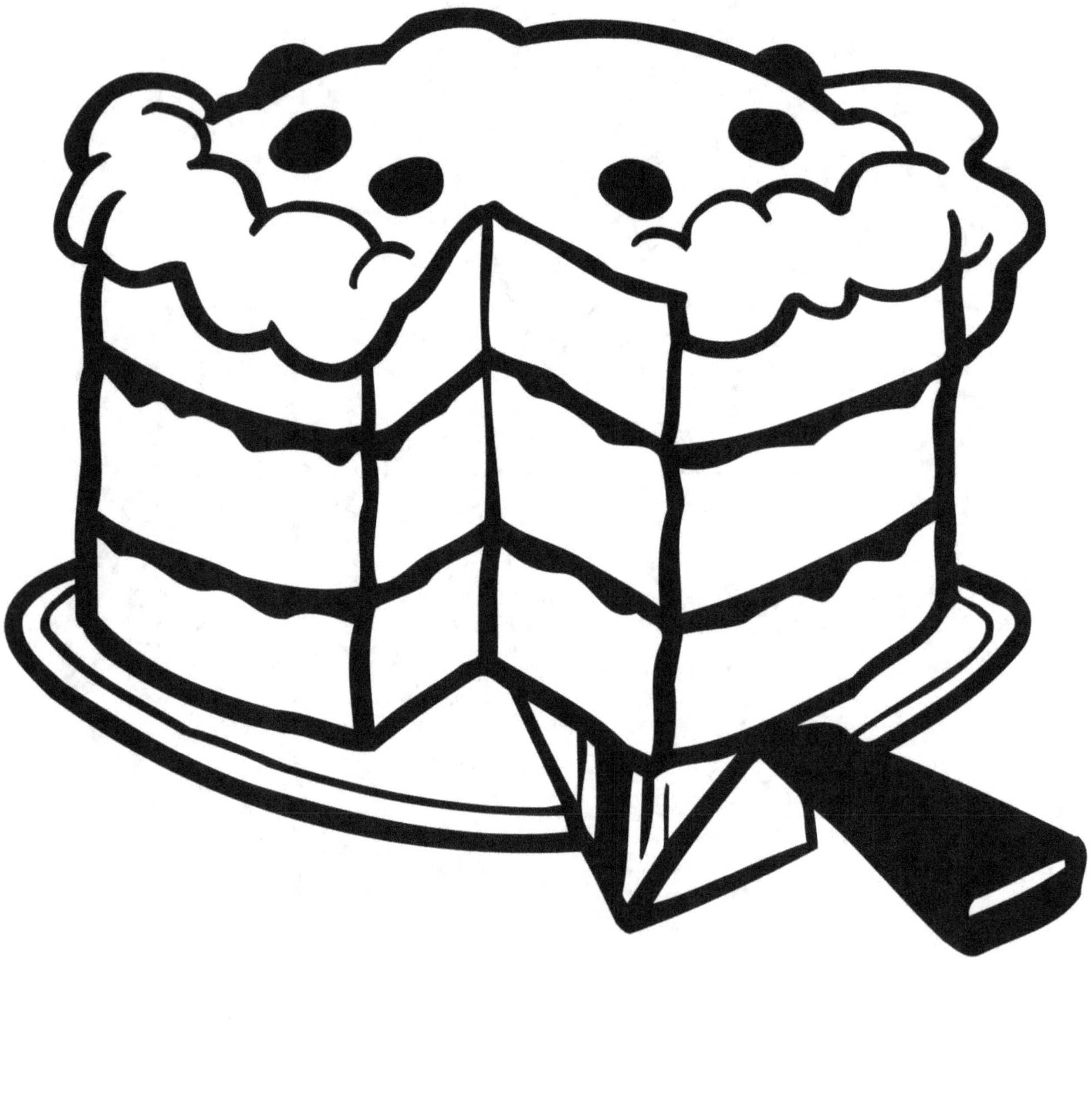

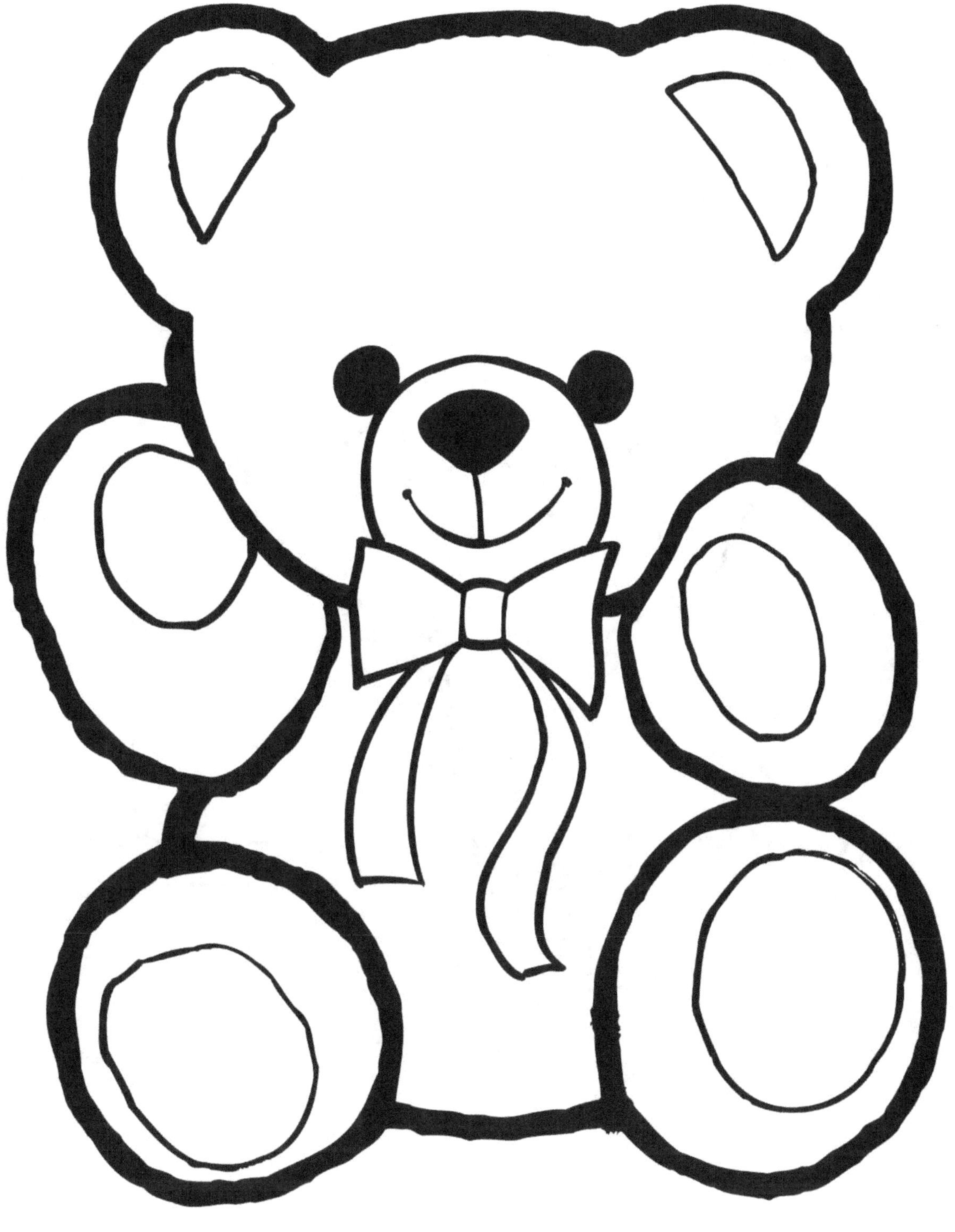

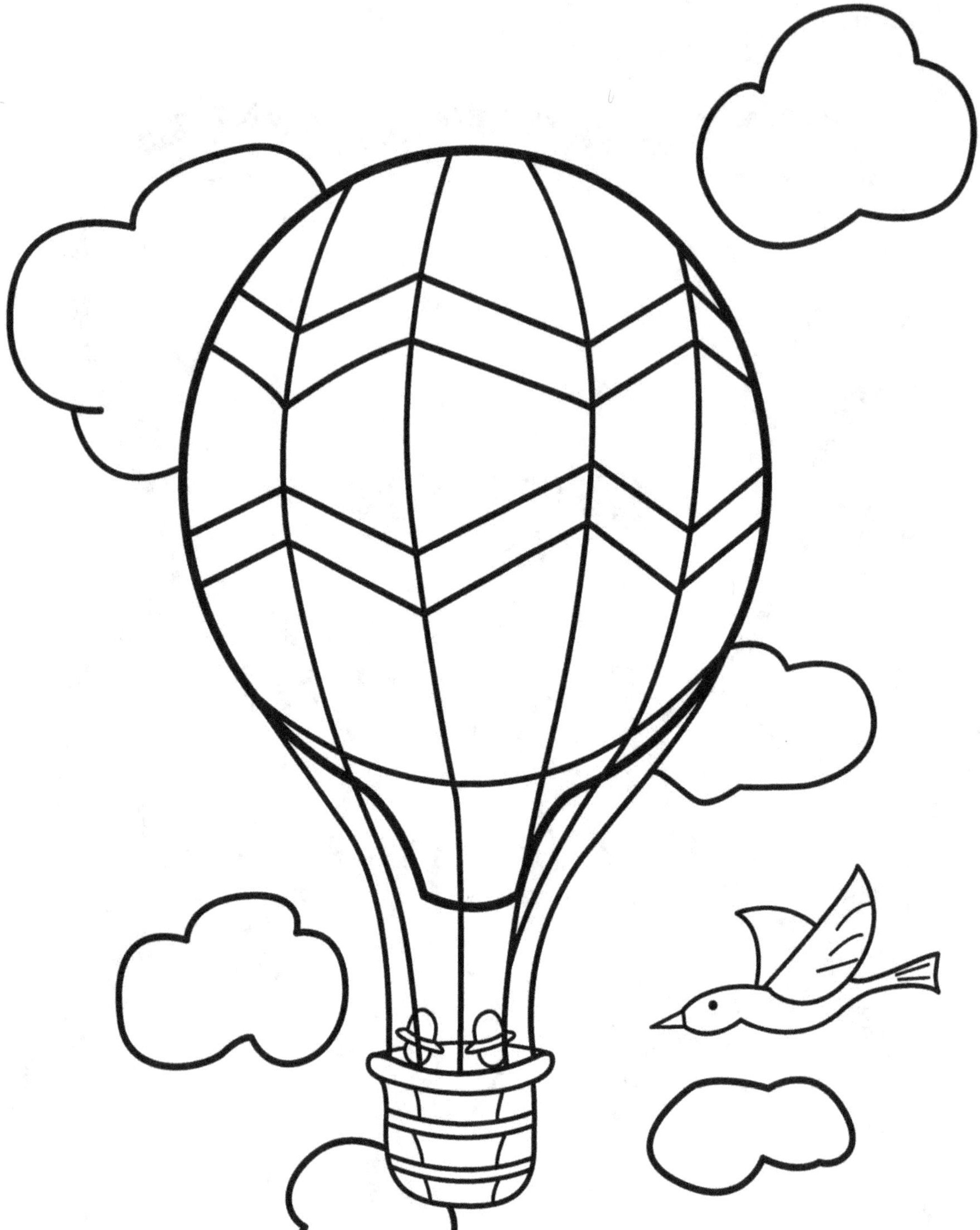

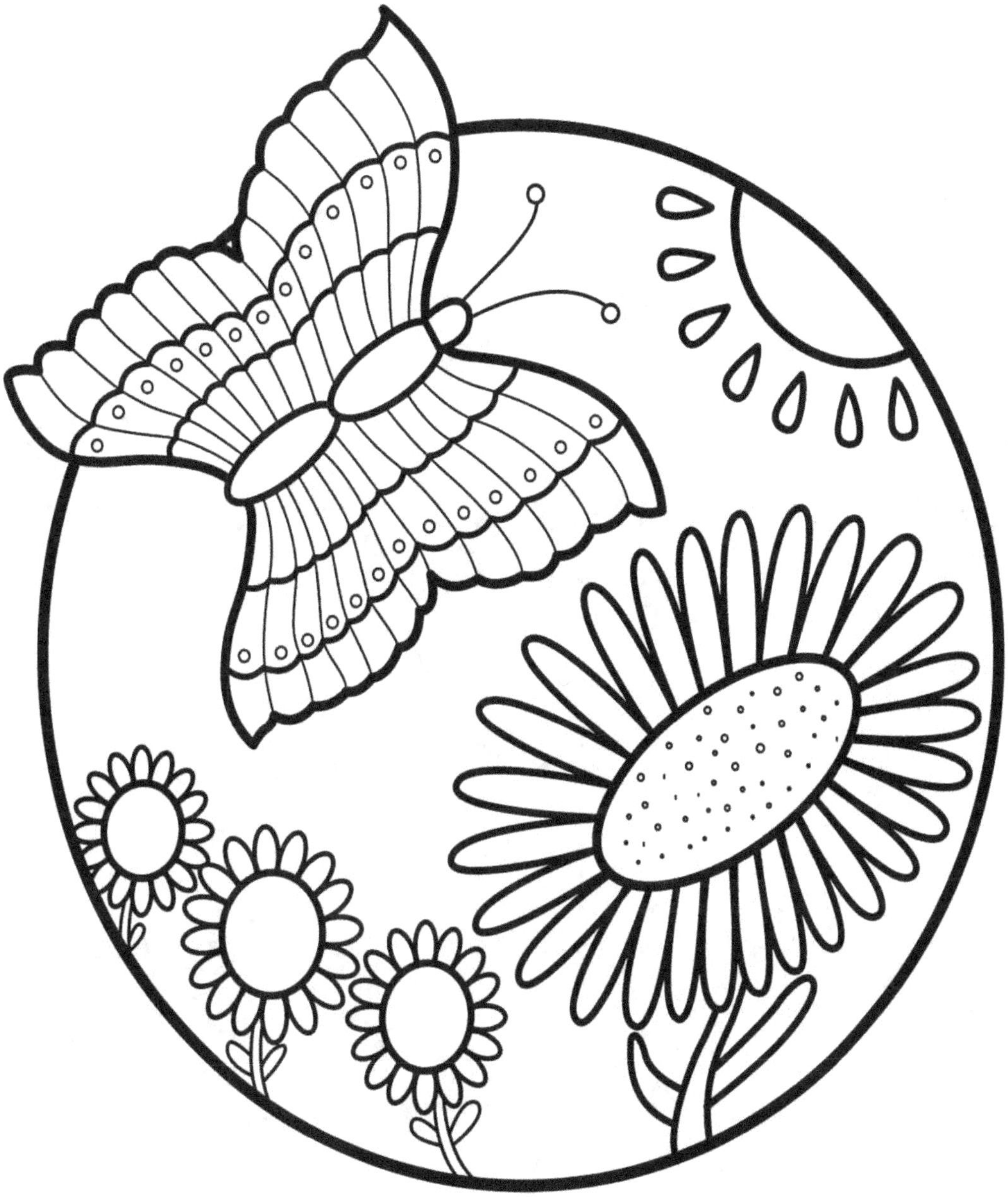

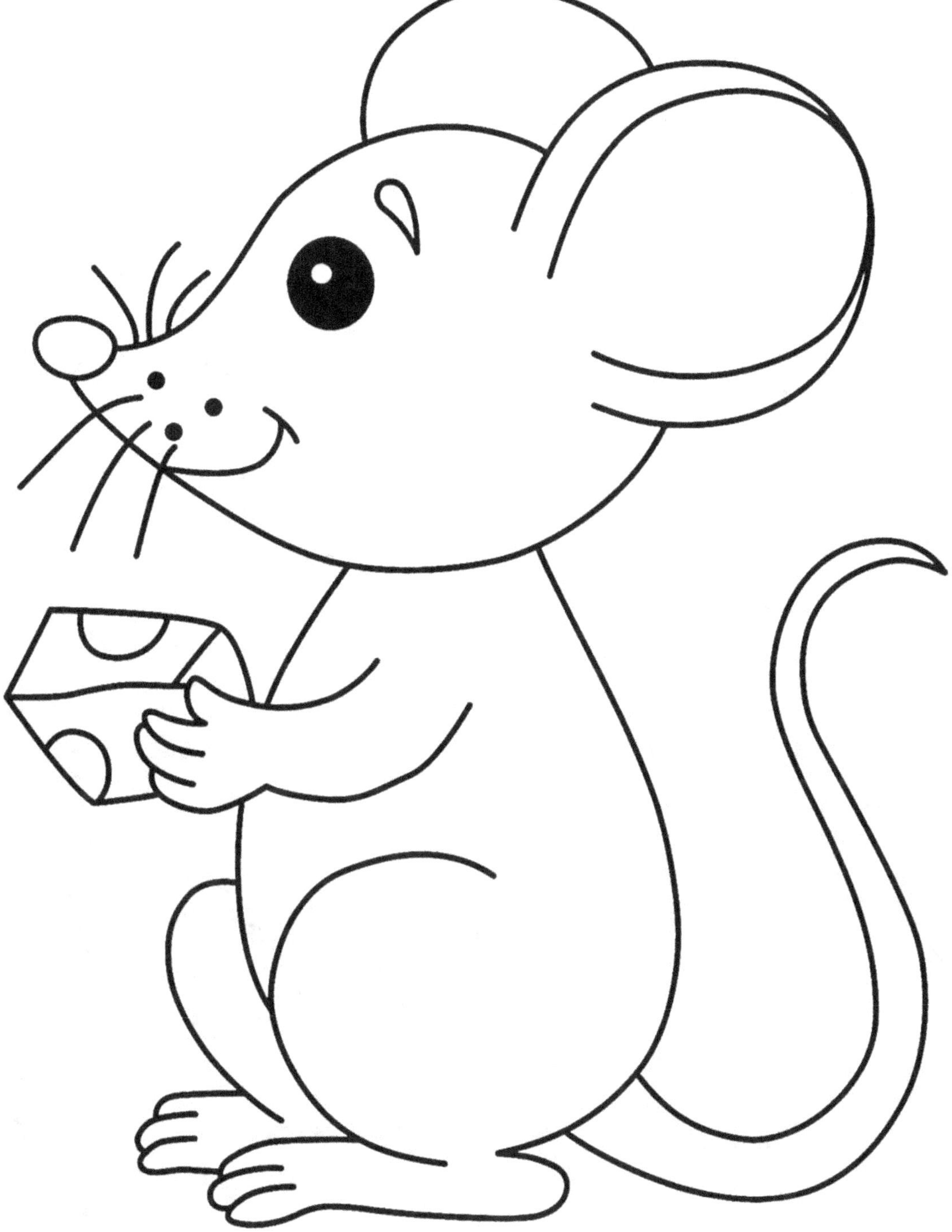

one 1	two 2
three 3	four 4

five 5	six 6
seven 7	eight 8

nine

9

zero

0

ten

10

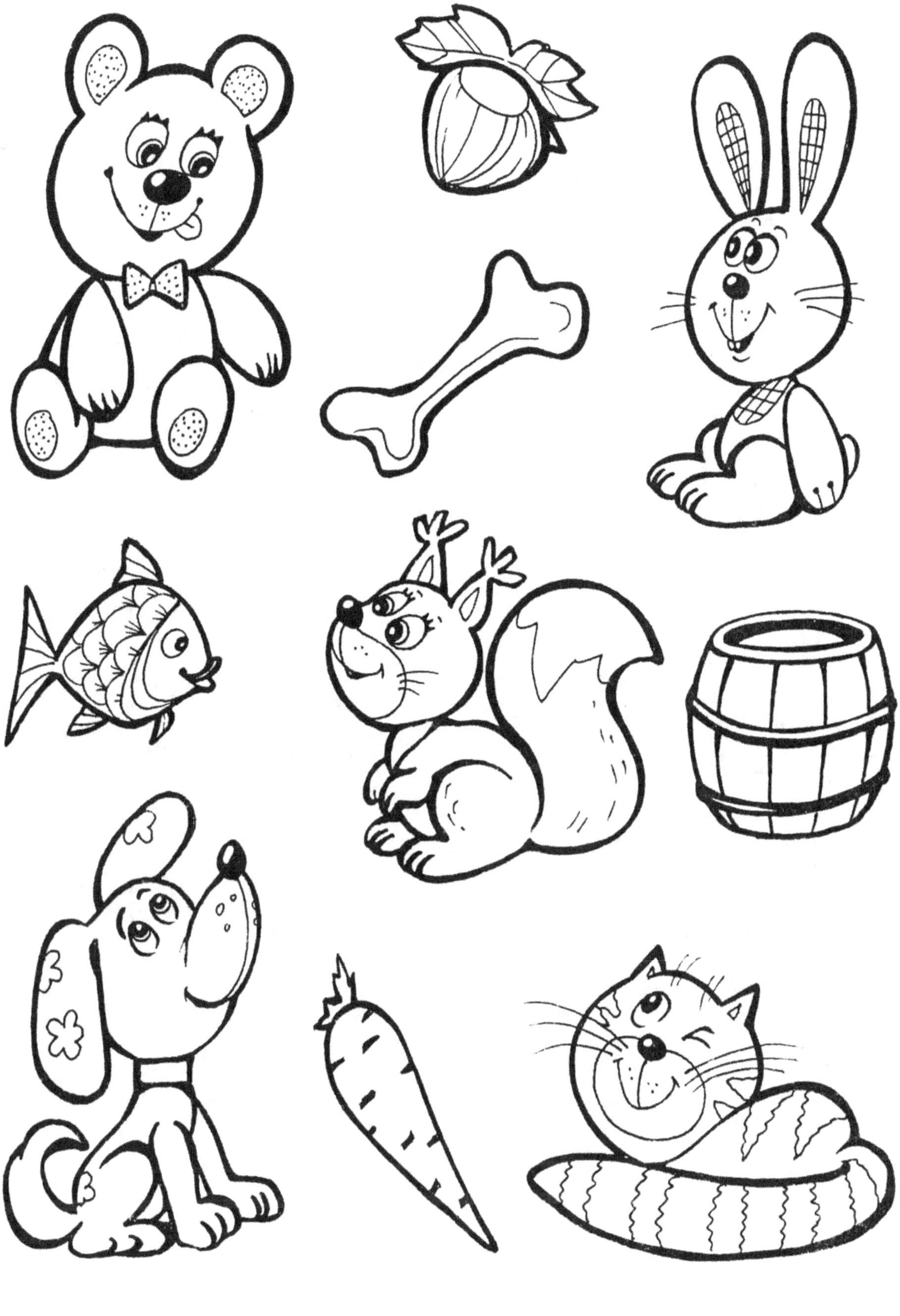

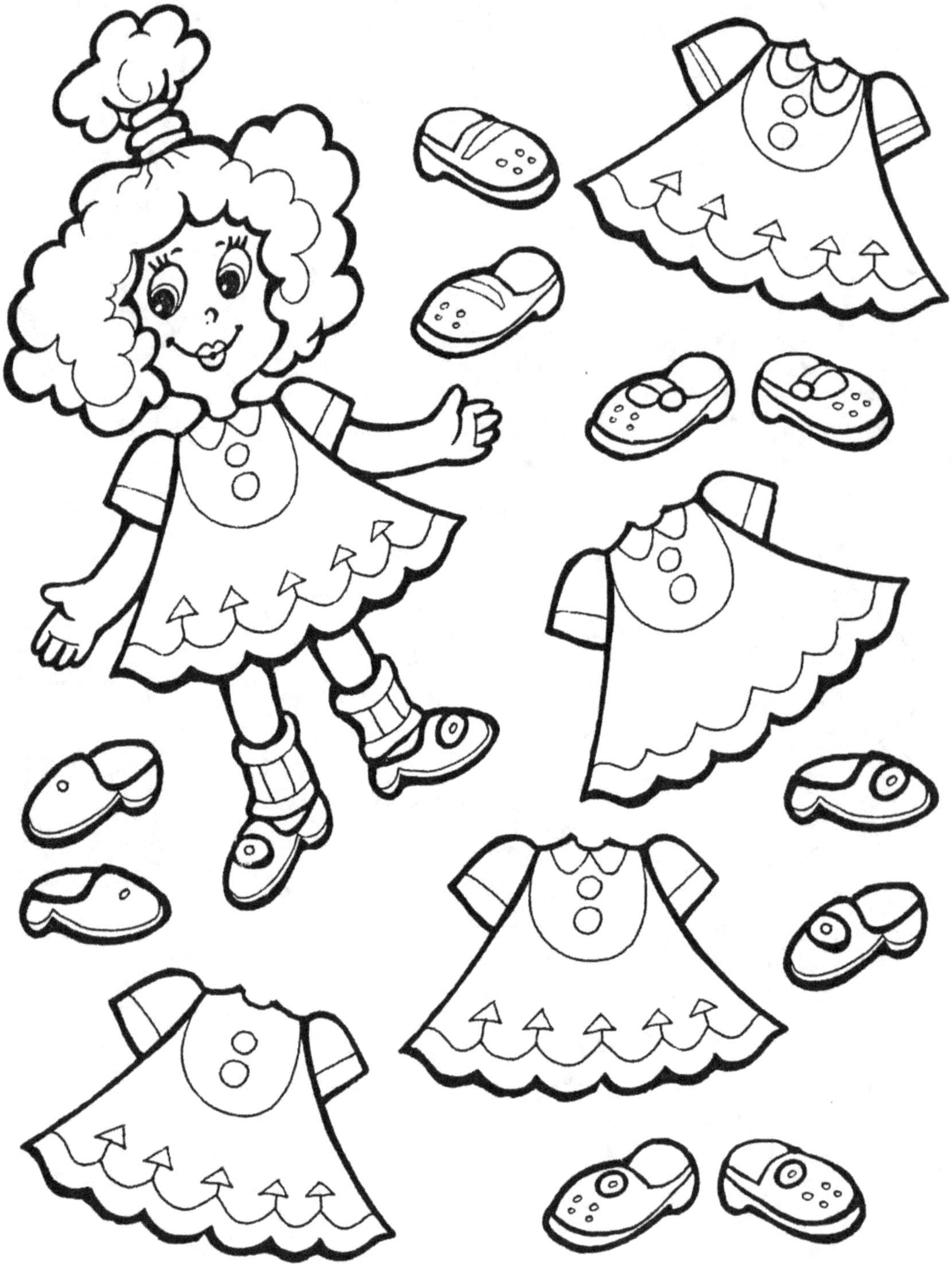

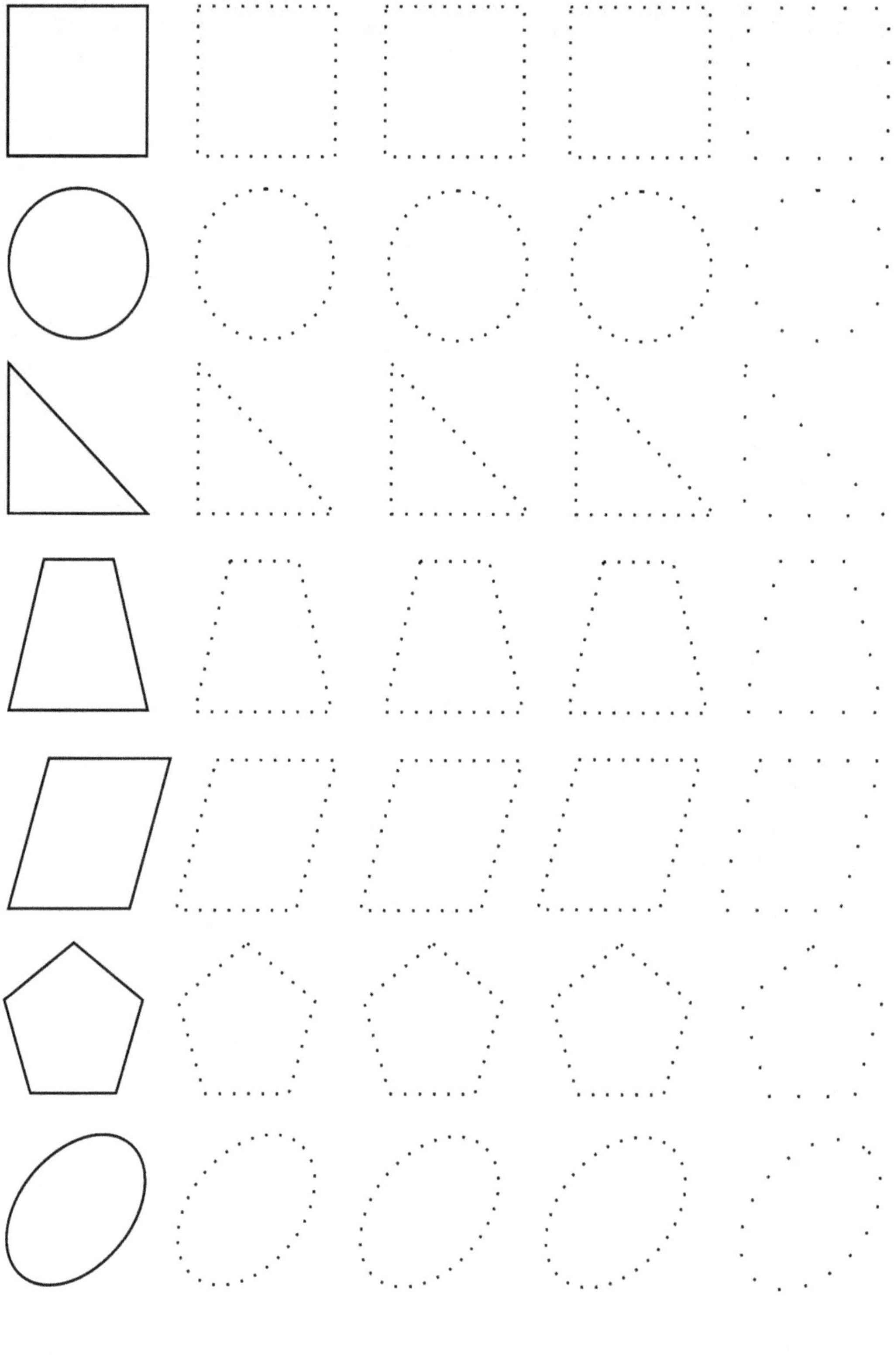

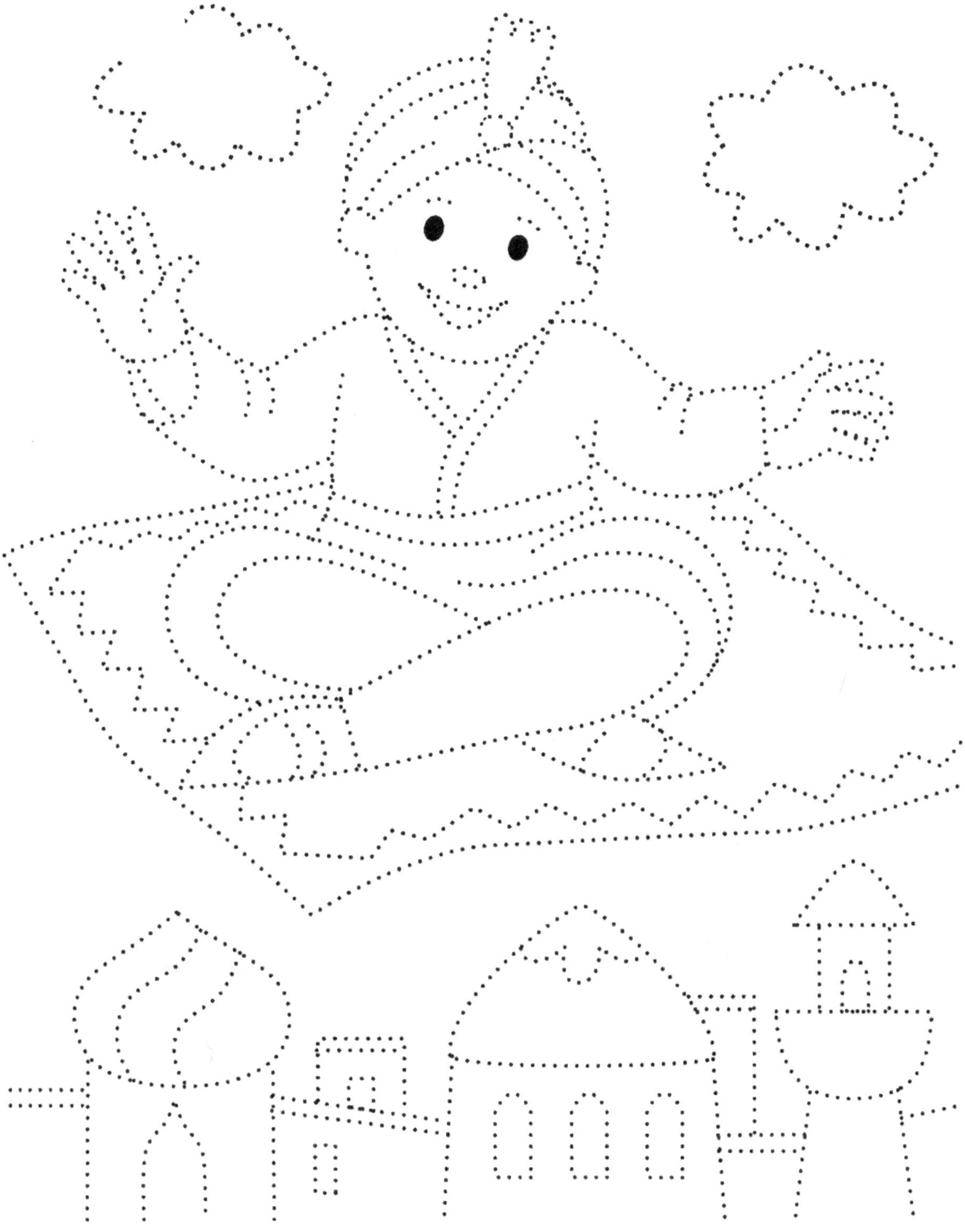

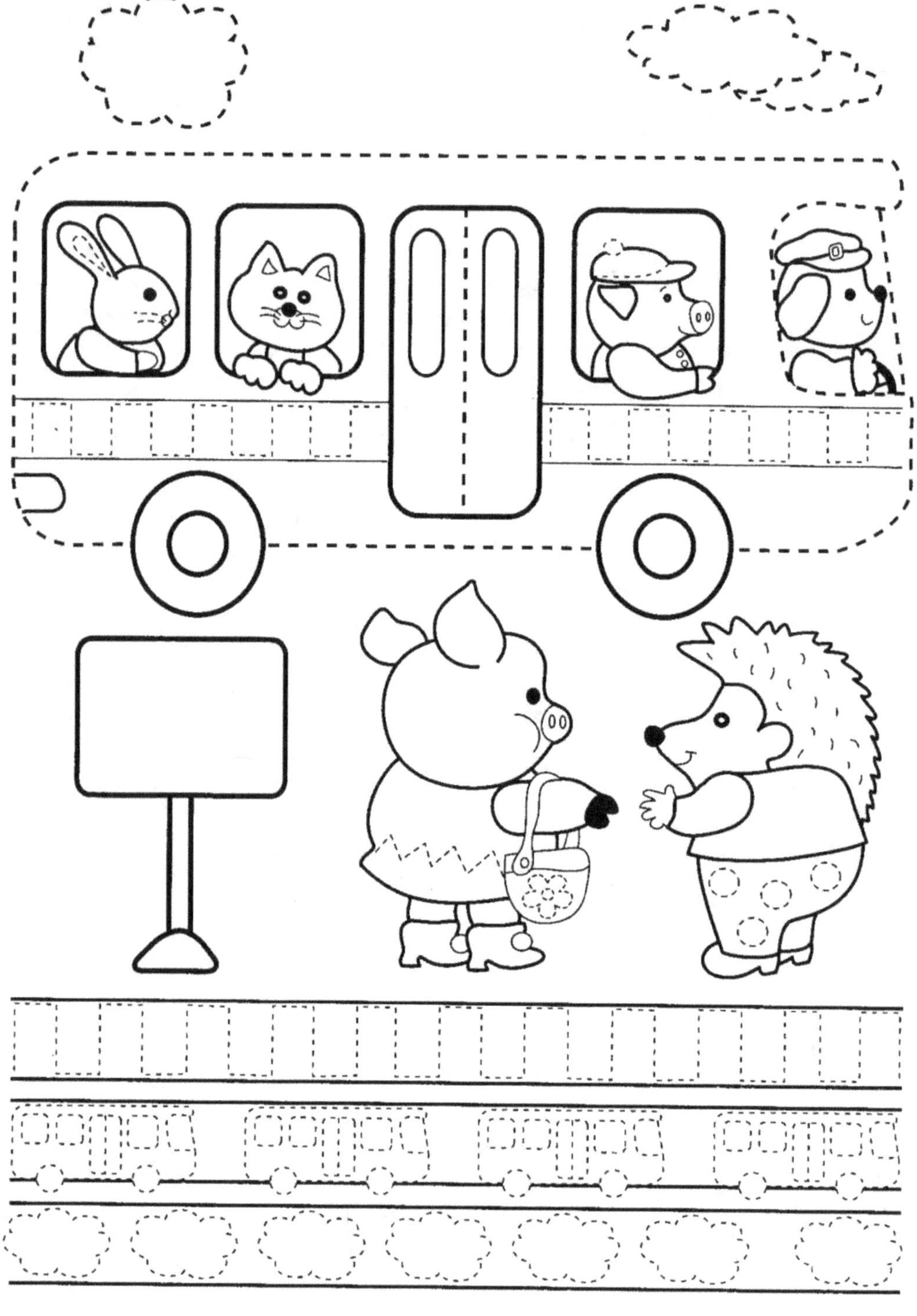

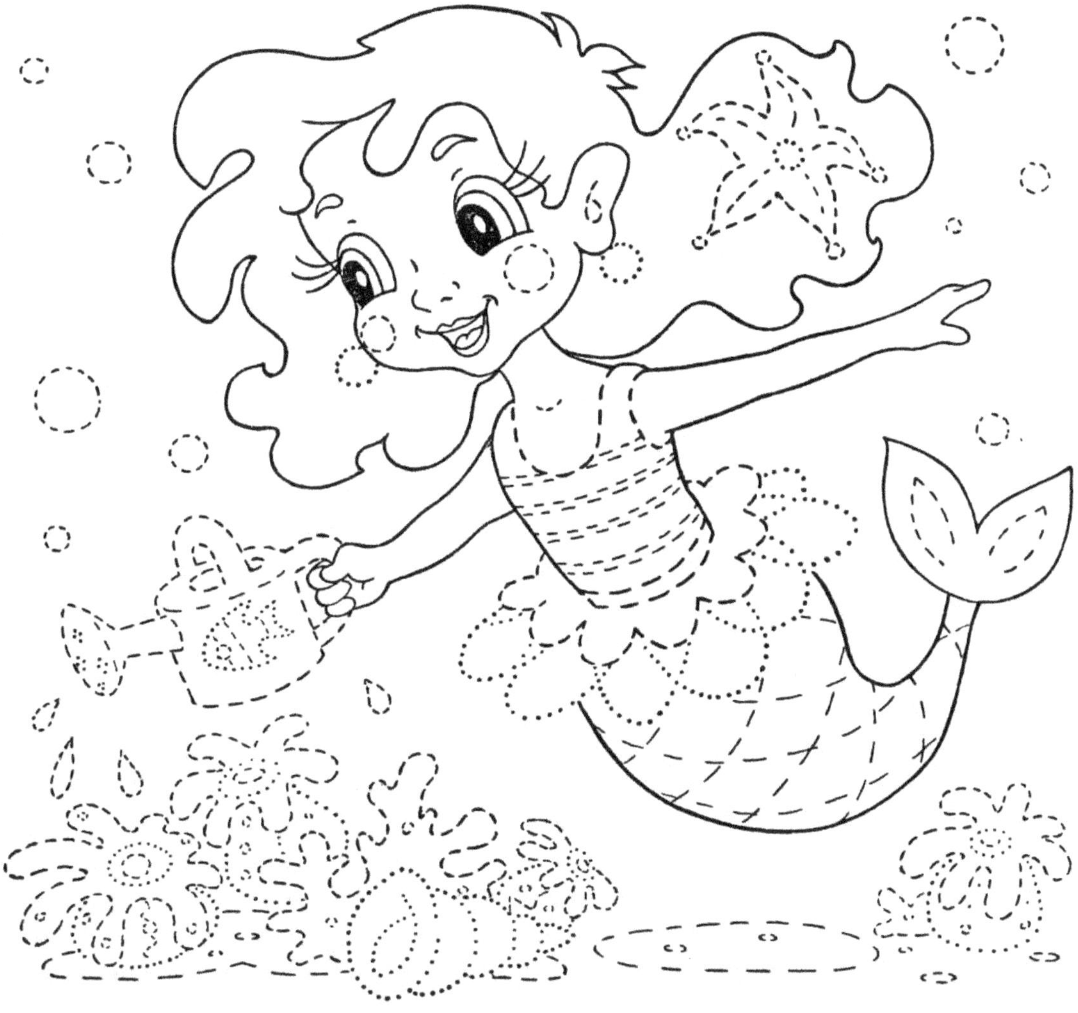

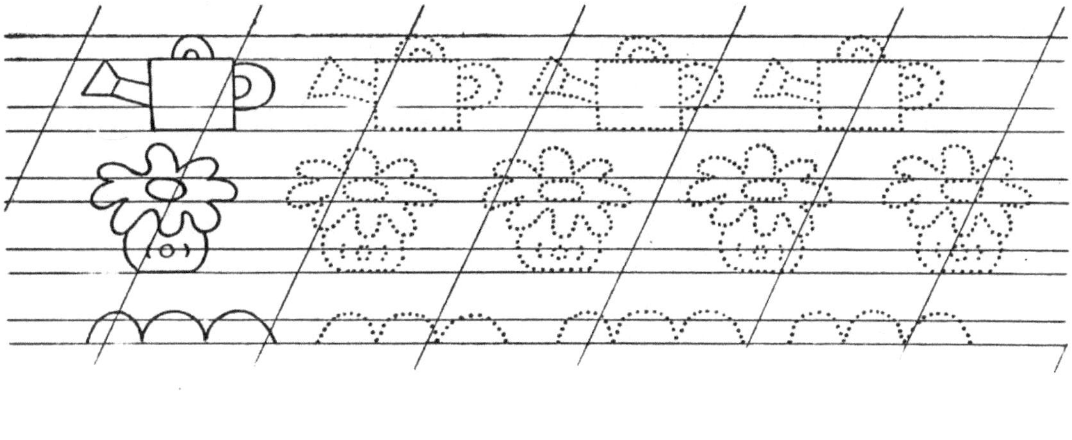

www.ingramcontent.com/pod-product-compliance
Lightning Source LLC
Chambersburg PA
CBHW081122240526
45470CB00019B/2917
9781979065283